CONTEÚDO DIGITAL PARA ALUNOS
Cadastre-se e transforme seus estudos em uma experiência única de aprendizado:

1 Entre na página de cadastro:
www.editoradobrasil.com.br/sistemas/cadastro

2 Além dos seus dados pessoais e de sua escola, adicione ao cadastro o código do aluno, que garantirá a exclusividade do seu ingresso a plataforma.

```
1020121A1234725
```

3 Depois, acesse: **www.editoradobrasil.com.br/leb**
e navegue pelos conteúdos digitais de sua coleção :D

Lembre-se de que esse código, pessoal e intransferível, é valido por um ano. Guarde-o com cuidado, pois é a única maneira de você utilizar os conteúdos da plataforma.

RENATO MENDES CURTO JÚNIOR
- Bacharel em Letras – Português e Inglês
- Especialista em Gestão e Docência
- Diplomado em proficiência pela *Michigan University* e pela *Indiana University* – Toefl

MARIANA CARDIERI MENDONÇA
- Professora de inglês da rede particular de ensino
- Diplomada com *First Certificate in English*, pela Cambridge e pelo Toefl

APOEMA
INGLÊS
6

1ª edição
São Paulo, 2018

Dados Internacionais de Catalogação na Publicação (CIP)
(Câmara Brasileira do Livro, SP, Brasil)

Curto Júnior, Renato Mendes
    Apoema: inglês 6 / Renato Mendes Curto Júnior, Mariana Cardieri Mendonça. – 1. ed. – São Paulo: Editora do Brasil, 2018. – (Coleção apoema)

    ISBN 978-85-10-06950-2 (aluno)
    ISBN 978-85-10-06951-9 (professor)

    1. Inglês (Ensino fundamental) I. Mendonça, Mariana Cardieri. II. Título. III. Série.

18-20210   CDD-372.652

Índices para catálogo sistemático:
1. Inglês: Ensino fundamental 372.652
Maria Alice Ferreira – Bibliotecária – CRB-8/7964

1ª edição / 5ª impressão, 2022
Impresso na Ricargraf

Rua Conselheiro Nébias, 887
São Paulo, SP – CEP 01203-001
Fone: +55 11 3226-0211
www.editoradobrasil.com.br

© Editora do Brasil S.A., 2018
Todos os direitos reservados

Direção geral: Vicente Tortamano Avanso

Direção editorial: Felipe Ramos Poleti
Gerência editorial: Erika Caldin
Supervisão de arte e editoração: Cida Alves
Supervisão de revisão: Dora Helena Feres
Supervisão de iconografia: Léo Burgos
Supervisão de digital: Ethel Shuña Queiroz
Supervisão de controle de processos editoriais: Marta Dias Portero
Supervisão de direitos autorais: Marilisa Bertolone Mendes

Supervisão editorial: Carla Felix Lopes
Edição: Amanda Leal e Monika Kratzer
Assistência editorial: Ana Okada e Juliana Pavoni
Auxiliar editorial: Beatriz Villanueva
Coordenação de revisão: Otacilio Palareti
Copidesque: Ricardo Liberal e Sylmara Beletti
Revisão: Alexandra Resende
Pesquisa iconográfica: Isabela Meneses
Assistência de arte: Samira de Souza
Design gráfico: Anexo Produção Editorial
Capa: Megalo Design
Ilustrações: Christiane S Messias, Cristiane Viana, Daniel Klein, Danillo Souza, Ilustra Cartoon, Kau Bispo, Leo Gibran, Luiz Lentini, Marcelo Azalim, Marcos De Mello, Marcos Guilherme, Ronaldo Barata, Tom B e Wasteresley Lima
Coordenação de editoração eletrônica: Abdonildo José de Lima Santos
Editoração eletrônica: Anderson Campos, Gilvan Alves da Silva e Sérgio Rocha
Licenciamentos de textos: Cinthya Utiyama, Jennifer Xavier, Paula Harue Tozaki e Renata Garbellini
Produção fonográfica: Jennifer Xavier e Cinthya Utiyama
Controle de processos editoriais: Bruna Alves, Carlos Nunes, Jefferson Galdino, Rafael Machado e Stephanie Paparella

HEY, STUDENT! WELCOME TO APOEMA!

A língua inglesa está cada vez mais presente nos nossos dias, seja na internet, na escola ou no trabalho. Tiramos *selfies* para postar nas redes sociais, levamos o *dog* para passear e fazemos a *homework* da escola, assistimos aos *youtubers* favoritos, vemos nossas séries e ouvimos nossas músicas em plataformas de *streaming* entre tantas outras coisas.

O conhecimento desta língua estrangeira é essencial para que possamos conhecer novos mundos, ampliar nossos horizontes e estarmos conectados com o que acontece ao nosso redor e no mundo. Por isso, é importante, e também gratificante, conhecer essa língua que conecta o mundo todo, compreender as culturas das quais ela faz parte.

Pensando nisso, nesta nova versão do **Apoema**, palavra da língua tupi que significa "aquele que vê mais longe", nosso objetivo não é apenas ensinar a língua estrangeira, mas também apresentar os diferentes lugares e culturas em que o inglês é o idioma nativo.

Nossa proposta é apresentar a língua inglesa de forma dinâmica, atual, interessante e ligada ao mundo real para que você possa usá-la para se comunicar, entendê-la e escrevê-la de forma fluente, interagindo com o mundo e expandindo seus horizontes, ou seja, vendo mais longe.

LET'S GET DOWN TO WORK!

Rawpixel.com/Shutterstock.com

SUMÁRIO

Unit 1 – What's your name?

Chapter 1	Let's practice – Parts of the name	8
	Let's listen n' speak – Greetings	9
	Let's practice – Greetings	10
Chapter 2	Let's practice – Personal pronouns	11
	Language piece – Present simple (to be)	12 e 13
	Vocabulary hint – Contractions	12
	Let's listen n' speak – Numbers 0 to 20	14
Chapter 3	Let's read n' write – Personal documents	15 a 17
Chapter 4	Tying in – Brazilian Sign Language (BSL) – Libras	18
	Project – Sign Language Greeting Guide	19

Unit 2 – Who are they?

Chapter 1	Let's practice – Family members	22 e 23
	Let's listen n' speak – Movie review: The Croods	24
Chapter 2	Language piece – Wh-question words	25 e 26
	Let's listen n' speak – My hat, it has three corners	27
	Language piece – Possessive adjectives	27
	Vocabulary hint – Possessives	28
Chapter 3	Let's read n' write – Movie Poster	29 a 31
Chapter 4	Citizenship moment – Family rules	32
	Project – Class rules	33

Review	34 e 35
Do not forget!	36
Overcoming challenges	37

Unit 3 – How is your routine?

Chapter 1	Let's practice – Daily activities	40 e 41
	Language piece – Adverbs of frequency	41
	Let's listen n' speak – Why having a daily routine is important?	42
Chapter 2	Language piece – Present simple	43 e 44
	Vocabulary hint – Verb ending in the Present simple	43
	Let's listen n' speak – Daily activities	46
Chapter 3	Let's read n' write – Personal Routine Comic strip	47 a 49
Chapter 4	Citizenship moment – What is responsibility?	50
	Project – Responsibility Chart	51

Unit 4 – Where are they from?

Chapter 1	Let's practice – Countries	54
	Let's listen n' speak – Landmarks	55 e 56
	Language piece – Question words	56
	Language piece – Question words	57
	Let's practice – Nationalities and languages	57 e 58
Chapter 2	Let's listen n' speak – Possessive case (Genitive)	59
	Language piece – Numbers: ordinal x cardinal	60
Chapter 3	Let's read n' write – Country facts form	61 a 63
Chapter 4	Tying in – World Continents	64
	Project – My country's curiosities	65

Review	66 e 67
Do not forget!	68
Overcoming challenges	69

Unit 5 – What are you doing?

Chapter 1	**Let's practice** – Leisure activities and hobbies	72 e 73
	Let's listen n' speak – Leisure activities	73 e 74
	Language piece – Play x Go x Do	74
Chapter 2	**Language piece** – Present continuous	75 a 77
	Vocabulary hint – /-ing/ sounds	75
	Let's listen n' speak – What are they doing?	78
Chapter 3	**Let's read n' write** – Summer Camp poster	79 a 81
Chapter 4	**Citizenship moment** – Scouts	82
	Project – Scouts	83

Unit 6 – What type of house is it?

Chapter 1	**Let's practice** – Types of houses	86
	– Parts of the house	87
	Let's listen n' speak – Parts of the house	88
Chapter 2	**Let's practice** – Objects of the house	89 a 91
	Language piece – There is x There are	90
	– Prepositions of place	91
	Vocabulary hint – Linking sounds	91
	Let's listen n' speak – Describing rooms	92
Chapter 3	**Let's read n' write** – Classified ad: house rental	93 a 95
Chapter 4	**Tying in** – Have you ever heard of EARTH HOUSES?	96
	Project – Sustainable materials	97

Review	98 e 99
Do not forget!	100
Overcoming challenges	101

Unit 7 – Who are they?

Chapter 1	**Let's practice** – Pet animals, wild animals and domestic animals	104
	Let's listen n' speak – Animal Facts	105 e 106
	Language piece – Opposite adjectives	107 e 108
Chapter 2	**Let's listen n' speak** – At the zoo	109
	Language piece – Demonstratives	110
	Vocabulary hint – Demonstratives	110
Chapter 3	**Let's read n' write** – Endangered species poster	111 a 113
	Language piece – Conjunctions	113
Chapter 4	**Citizenship moment** – Western Lowland Gorilla Slipping out of Existence	114
	Project – Research: Brazilian endangered species	115

Unit 8 – What day is today?

Chapter 1	**Let's practice** – Seasons of the year	118
	– Months of the year	118
	Let's listen n' speak – Four seasons	119 e 120
Chapter 2	**Let's practice** – Days of the week	121
	Language piece – Telling the time	122
	Vocabulary hint – Time expressions	122
	Let's listen n' speak – Describing appointments	123
	Language piece – Prepositions of time	124
Chapter 3	**Let's read n' write** – School week planner	125 a 127
Chapter 4	**Tying in** – Time zone	128
	Project – Brazilian Time Zones	129

Review	130 e 131
Do not forget!	132
Overcoming challenges	133

Workbook	134 a 149
Expert's Point	150 a 153
I. The "Do You Know?" 20 Questions About Family Stories	150 e 151
II. Scientists Say: Zooplankton	152 e 153

Focus on culture	154 a 157
I. Housing, Health and Scholar Performance	154 e 155
II. Pets and Homes in Brazil	156 e 157
Language Court	158 a 169
Glossary	170 a 175

UNIT 1
WHAT'S YOUR NAME?

Wall-E.

Stich and Lilo.

Eunice and Mavis.

||| Get ready |||

1 Look at the pictures. What are people doing?

a) ◯ They are greeting each other.

b) ◯ They are having fun with each other.

2 What do you say when you meet a person? Check all possibilities.

a) ◯ Hi!

b) ◯ So long.

c) ◯ Hello!

d) ◯ How are you?

e) ◯ Goodbye!

f) ◯ Nice to meet you.

3 Do you know all these greetings? Label each picture with the correct greeting.

kiss • wave • handshake • hug

Vanellope von Schweetz and Ralph.

CHAPTER 1

Let's practice

1 How many parts does a name have? Look at the celebrities' names and complete the table.

a)
Hello, I'm Destiny Hope Cyrus. My nickname is Miley.

b)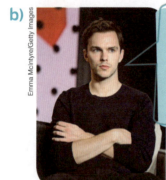
Hi, my name is Nicholas Caradoc Hoult. You can call me Nick.

c)
Hi, my name is Amethyst Amelia Kelly. You can call me Iggy Azalea.

d)
Hello, I'm Aubrey Drake Graham. My nickname is Drake.

First name	Second name (middle name)	Last name (surname)	Nickname
	Hope		
Nicholas			
		Kelly	
			Drake
You			

LANGUAGE PIECE

Full name: **Maria Eduarda Carvalho.**
First name: **Maria.**
Second / Middle Name: **Eduarda.**
Last Name / Surname: **Carvalho.**
Nickname: **Duda.**

8

Let's listen n' speak

1 Listen to the people greeting each other. Complete the greetings with the appropriate words.

afternoon • morning • evening • night

a)
- Good _____, honey.
  Time to get up.

b)
- Good _____, girls.
  Sweet dreams.

c)
- Good _____, mom.
  How are you?

d)
- Good _____!
  Thank you.

2 Let's learn other greetings. Choose the best option to each image.

a)
- ◯ Hi!   • ◯ Goodbye!

c)
- ◯ I'm just fine, thanks!   • ◯ I'm not ok.

b)
- ◯ I'm just fine, thanks!   • ◯ I'm not ok.

d)
- ◯ Hello!   • ◯ Bye!

Let's practice

1 Choose the best greeting to complete the dialogues.

> Hi • Good night • Good afternoon • Nice to meet you, too

a) "_____, kids! My name is Mr. Hanks."

"Good afternoon, Mr. Hanks!"

b) "I'm going to bed. _____"

"_____, sweetie."

c) "Hello, aunt Mary!"

"_____, Ben! How are you?"

d) "Nice to meet you, Albert!"

"_____"

2 Write the greetings according to the images.

a)
_____

b)
_____

c)
_____

d)
_____

3 Which is the correct greeting: **Good night!** or **Good evening!**

a)

b)

_____ _____

CHAPTER 2

Let's practice

1 Look at the scenes.

Paul Sanders

Abby Ibsen

Kevin Tanaka

I am Paul Sanders.

You are my friend.

She is my friend.

He is my friend.

We are friends.

They are classmates and friends.

This is my dog, Pingo.

Now, choose the best option.

a) Abby Ibsen
- ( ) He is Paul's friend.
- ( ) She is Paul's friend.

b) Kevin Tanaka
- ( ) He is Paul's friend.
- ( ) She is Paul's friend.

c) Paul, Abby and Kevin
- ( ) They are friends.
- ( ) We are friends.

d) Paul and I
- ( ) They are friends.
- ( ) We are friends.

e) Pingo

- ◯ It is a dog.
- ◯ He is a dog.

f) Which is correct?

- ◯ I am.
- ◯ I are.

2 Write the correct subject pronoun.

a) Paul and I _____

b) Paul, Abby and Kevin _____

c) Abby _____

d) Kevin _____

3 Complete the exercises with **am**, **is** or **are**.

a) I _____ your friend.

b) Lily and Bob _____ good friends.

c) Snowflake _____ my pet.

LANGUAGE PIECE

To be – affirmative form

I am	→	I'm
You are	→	You're
He is	→	He's
She is	→	She's
It is	→	It's
We are	→	We're
You are	→	You're
They are	→	They're

4 Take a look.

We are not brothers.

It is not a cat.

Now, complete the sentences using **am not**, **is not** or **are not**.

a) Carol and Yuki _____ teachers.

b) I _____ a doctor.

c) His sister _____ ten years old.

Vocabulary hint
Contractions

I'm	You're
He's	She's
It's	You're
We're	They're

TRACK 02

LANGUAGE PIECE

To be – negative form

I am not	→	I'm not
You are not	→	You aren't
He is not	→	He isn't
She is not	→	She isn't
It is not	→	It isn't
We are not	→	We aren't
You are not	→	You aren't
They are not	→	They aren't

Ilustrações: Kau Bispo

5. **Complete the questions with are or is.**

Are they your friends?

Is it your cat?

a) _____ Matthew and Peter brothers?

b) _____ Maria your friend?

c) _____ the kids in the classroom?

d) _____ your dog around here?

e) _____ I your cousin?

f) _____ we neighbors?

6. **Write sentences using the verb to be as indicated.**

a) I / hungry – (negative)

_____

b) Carol and Yuki / the new classmates – (interrogative)

_____

c) Christian / 6th grader – (interrogative)

_____

d) My grandfather / Russian – (affirmative)

_____

e) The weather / good – (negative)

_____

f) Taylor / singer – (affirmative)

_____

LANGUAGE PIECE

To be – interrogative form

Am I …?	**Is** it …?
Are you …?	**Are** you …?
Is he …?	**Are** we …?
Is she …?	**Are** they …?

Let's listen n' speak

1 Listen to part A, complete the table and repeat.

two • nine • six • four • fifteen • nineteen • twelve • zero

0	1	2	3	4	5	6
	one		three		five	
7	8	9	10	11	12	13
seven	eight		ten	eleven		thirteen
14	15	16	17	18	19	20
fourteen		sixteen	seventeen	eighteen		twenty

2 Now, listen to part B and answer the questions.

a) How many boys are there?
- ◯ Seven.
- ◯ Three.

b) How many girls are there?
- ◯ Nine.
- ◯ One.

c) How many desks are there?
- ◯ Twelve.
- ◯ Twenty.

d) How many students are on the bus?
- ◯ Sixteen.
- ◯ Eight.

3 How old are they?

a)  10 How old is the girl?

_____

c)  8 How old is the boy?

_____

e)  9 How old is the girl?

_____

b)  12 How old is the boy?

_____

d)  15 How old is the girl?

_____

f)  20 How old is the boy?

_____

CHAPTER 3

Let's read n' write

1 Look at the images and answer the questions.

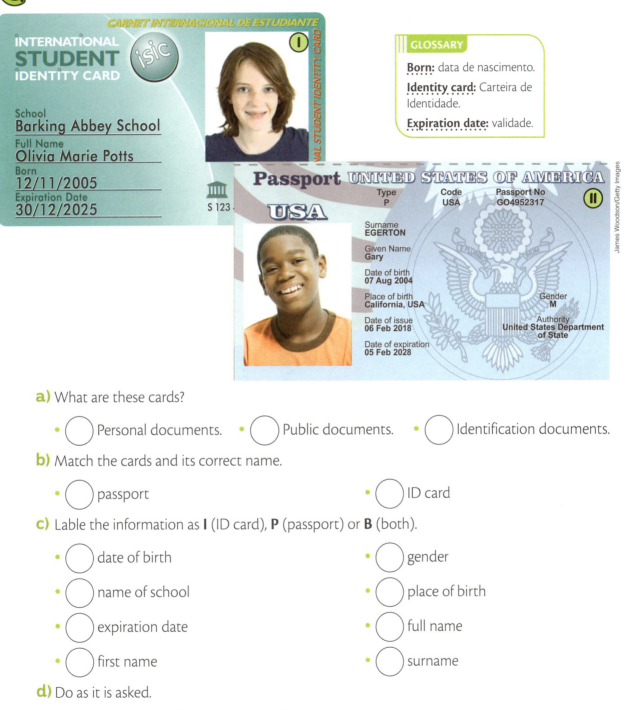

a) What are these cards?

- ◯ Personal documents.
- ◯ Public documents.
- ◯ Identification documents.

GLOSSARY

Born: data de nascimento.
Identity card: Carteira de Identidade.
Expiration date: validade.

b) Match the cards and its correct name.

- ◯ passport
- ◯ ID card

c) Lable the information as **I** (ID card), **P** (passport) or **B** (both).

- ◯ date of birth
- ◯ name of school
- ◯ expiration date
- ◯ first name
- ◯ gender
- ◯ place of birth
- ◯ full name
- ◯ surname

d) Do as it is asked.

- Circle with red the first names and with blue the surnames.
- Crossout with blue the years of birth.
- Underline with green the name of the school.
- Underline with orange the place of birth.

2 Why are these kinds of document important?
Because …

_____

3 Complete the ID cards with the correct information.

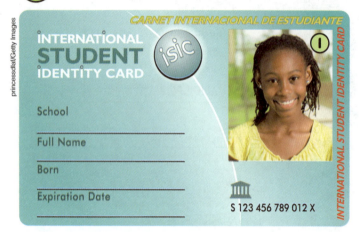

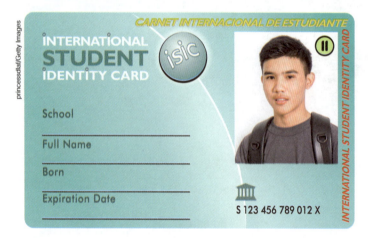

12/4/2028
Fernanda Silva
Matthew Chen
10/22/2000
Martin Jr. Middle School
5/15/2008
Virginia High School
12/4/2020

4 Look at the ID cards from exercise 3 and answer the questions.

a) When was Fernanda Silva born?

_____

b) What is the boy's name?

_____

c) Where does the girl study?

_____

d) What is the expiration date of the boy's ID card?

_____

5 What sort of information do the ID cards have? Check all possibilities.

a) ◯ Phone number.
b) ◯ School name.
c) ◯ Expiration date.
d) ◯ Occupation.
e) ◯ Name.
f) ◯ Parents' names.
g) ◯ Date of birth.
h) ◯ Address.
i) ◯ Photo.

6 Talk to your classmates.

- Do you have an ID card? Why is it important?
- Do you have a student ID card? If not, would you like to have one? Why?

7 Complete the ID card and the Passport with your personal information.

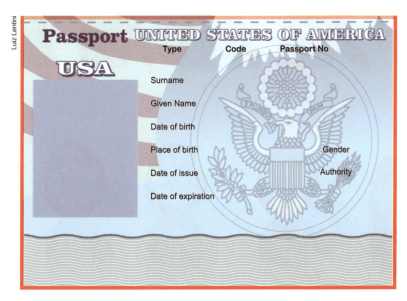

EXPLORING

Have fun creating your own ID card at:

- http://disneyjunior.disney.com/disney-junior-card-creator
- www.savethechildren.org/atf/cf/%7B9def2ebe-10ae-432c-9bd0-df91d2eba74a%7D/CHILDIDCARD.PDF

CHAPTER 4

||| Tying in |||

Brazilian Sign Language (BSL) – Libras

Sign language is a language that uses hand and body movements to represent words and convey meaning. It is used by and for people who cannot hear or talk. There are different types of sign languages all around the world, such as the Brazilian Sign Language, called Libras, and the American Sign Language.

Check some greetings used in Libras.

Hi! / Hello!

How are you?

I'm fine.

Nice to meet you.

Good morning.

Ilustrações: Leo Gibran

Good afternoon.

Good night.

Goodbye. / Bye.

Let's practice

1. **Pair up and role-play a short dialogue using the greetings in Libras. Have fun!**

2. **Let's play Chinese Whispers. Follow your teacher's instructions and have fun!**

EXPLORING

- *Saying what you mean: a children's book,* by Joy Wilt. Educational Prod. Division Word, Incorporated.

PROJECT

Sign Language Greeting Guide

Imagine your school is going to receive some visiting students from a foreign country. The foreign students can only communicate in Libras or ASL (American Sign Language). You and your classmates will have to create a paper guide to help the students from your school to greet the visitants.

UNIT 2

WHO ARE THEY?

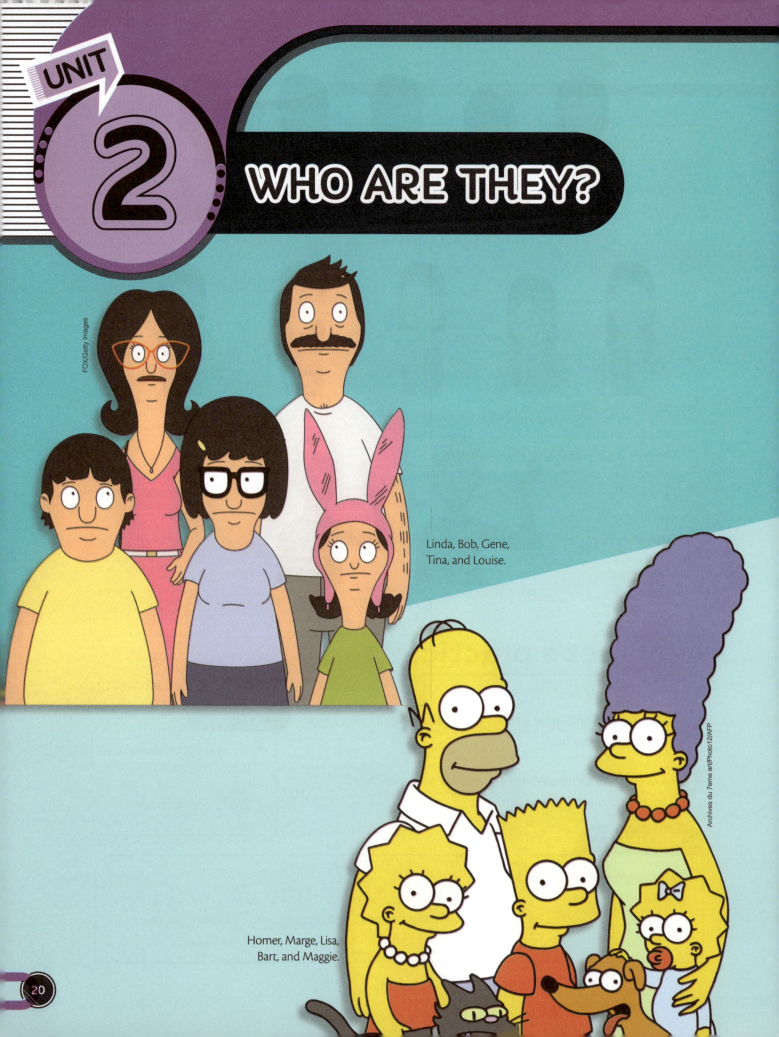

Linda, Bob, Gene, Tina, and Louise.

Homer, Marge, Lisa, Bart, and Maggie.

||| Get ready |||

1. Do you know the families in the pictures? Who are they?

2. Can you identify the members of each family? Complete the table.

Family member	Name
Father	
Mother	
Son	
Daugther	

3. What about your family: How many people are there? Who are they?

_____

_____

Gru, Lucy, Minions, Edith, Agnes, and Margo.

CHAPTER 1

Let's practice

1 Look at the family tree and write the family relationships.

> mother • father • sister • brother • cousin
> uncle • aunt • grandmother • grandfather

2 Look at the family tree from exercise 1 and complete the family relationships.

a) Liza is Victoria's _____.

b) John is Helena's _____.

c) Victoria is Isabella's _____.

d) Benjamin is Angela's _____.

e) Simon is Helena's, Timmy's, Benjamin's, and Angela's _____.

f) Philipe is Helena's _____.

g) Simon and Liza are Isabella's and Victoria's _____.

h) Philipe is Timmy's _____.

i) Isabella is Angela's _____.

j) Liza is Timmy's _____.

3 Unscramble the words and find out the family members.

a) ehfrta _____

b) ons _____

c) tuhgdare _____

d) tuan _____

e) gandetohrrm _____

f) scunoi _____

4 Who are they? Guess the correct family relationships.

a) Your mother's sister is your _____.

b) Your father's brother is your _____.

c) Your uncle's son is your _____.

d) Your dad's mother is your _____.

5 Word search. Find the name of ten family members in the word search.

V	N	J	V	S	I	S	T	E	R	R	I	F	I	L
G	R	A	N	D	M	O	T	H	E	R	B	A	M	D
Y	Y	R	U	N	C	L	E	A	J	G	R	T	O	W
W	N	H	T	C	O	Q	T	A	C	D	O	H	T	Y
A	D	H	I	X	R	A	U	N	T	G	T	E	H	Q
E	E	A	K	M	F	S	Q	P	D	U	H	R	E	F
R	J	A	U	E	A	Q	J	Y	P	L	E	L	R	C
M	J	Y	N	F	P	F	X	P	M	A	R	I	H	O
G	R	A	N	D	F	A	T	H	E	R	L	K	T	U
T	R	D	Y	V	R	T	J	P	A	Z	H	N	M	S
T	Q	T	A	U	M	O	E	D	G	Z	L	O	H	I
D	A	U	G	H	T	H	E	R	D	J	M	Q	I	N

23

Let's listen n' speak

1 Do you know *The Croods*? It is a movie about a caveman's family. Listen to the movie review and complete it with the missing information.

brother • daughter • grandma • sister • dad • family • mom

Movie Review: *The Croods*

The Croods is a story about a **caveman** _____ who lives in a **cave**. The **heroine** of this story is a **teenage** _____ called Eep, meaning **stone**. She lives with her **crazy** _____, Gran, her little baby _____, Sandy, her younger _____, Thunk, her _____, Ugga, and her **overprotective** _____, Grug!

GLOSSARY

Cave: caverna.
Caveman: homem das cavernas.
Crazy: louco(a).
Heroine: heroína.
Overprotective: superprotetor(a).
Stone: pedra.
Teenage: adolescente.

2 Now, answer some questions about *The Croods'* family.

a) Check all the family members mentioned.

- ◯ brother
- ◯ cousin
- ◯ father / dad
- ◯ grandmother
- ◯ mother / mom
- ◯ sister

b) Who are they? Complete with the family relationships.

- Ugga _____
- Thunk _____
- Sandy _____
- Eep _____
- Gran _____
- Grug _____

Let's practice

1 Let's learn more about *The Croods*.

Movies

Movie review: *The Croods*

The Croods is a **story** about a caveman family who live in a cave and they are the only humans on **Earth**. One night, Eep sees a **bright light** coming from **outside** the cave and she is **keen to follow** it.

GLOSSARY

Bright: brilhante.
Earth: Terra.
Keen: entusiasmado(a).
Light: luz.
Outside: do lado de fora.
Story: história.
To follow: seguir.

a) Match the questions with the answers.

- **What** is the story about?
- **Where** do they live?
- **Who** sees a bright light?

- Eep.
- They live in a cave.
- It is about a caveman family.

LANGUAGE PIECE

Wh-question words
What ⟶ thing
Who ⟶ person/people
Where ⟶ place
When ⟶ time

b) Circle using the correct color.

WHO   WHAT   WHERE

c) Who are they?

Gran, grandmother. • Sandy, baby sister. • Thunk, younger brother.

_____   _____   _____

25

d) **Where** do they live? Circle.

Tent.

Cave.

House.

e) **When** do you imagine the story takes place?

- ◯ Past.
- ◯ Present.
- ◯ Future.

2 Check the best option to each question. Use the pictures to help you out.

a) Who is in the bedroom?

- ◯ My cousin.
- ◯ My grandma.

c) What is on the table?

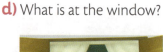

- ◯ A notebook.
- ◯ Three magazines.

e) Where do you live?

- ◯ In a house.
- ◯ In a building.

b) Where is his father?

- ◯ In the living room.
- ◯ In the garage.

d) What is at the window?

- ◯ Three books.
- ◯ A bird.

f) When does the sun come up?

- ◯ At night.
- ◯ In the morning.

3 Use the question words to ask information about your classmate's family. Take turns asking and answering.

Let's listen n' speak

1 Listen to a traditional child rhyme and follow the instructions.

MY HAT, IT HAS THREE CORNERS

My **hat**, it has three **corners**.
Three corners has my hat.
And had it not three corners,
it would not be my hat.

Traditional rhyme.

GLOSSARY

Corner: ponta, canto.

Hat: chapéu.

a) Circle the possessive adjective. What is it? _____

b) Who is the owner of the hat? _____

2 Let's test our knowledge! Rewrite the rhyme following the instructions.

a) Use **she** instead of **I**. Now, who is the owner of the hat?

_____
_____

LANGUAGE PIECE

Possessive adjectives

I – My	You – Your
He – His	She – Her
It – Its	We – Our
You – Your	They – Their

b) Use **they** instead of **I**. Now, who are the owners of the hat?

_____
_____
_____

3 In pairs, use your imagination and make a rhyme of your own using the possessive adjectives. Write it on your notebook and read it to your classmates.

27

Let's practice

1 What is the correct option? Complete the sentences with the possessive adjectives.

> my • our • your • his • their • its • her

a) Where is _____ backpack? (I)

b) Here is _____ teacher. (you)

c) _____ mother works at the City Hospital. (they)

d) _____ computer is very expensive. (we)

e) _____ favorite hobby is running. (he)

f) Leila likes _____ cat. _____ name is Fluffy. (she / it)

g) She goes to school with _____ cousin. (she)

h) _____ grandmother wants to travel to Hawaii. (I)

2 Circle the correct alternative.

a) Gabriel loves (his / her / its) school.

b) Tina and Lisa are in (our / your / their) gymnastics class right now.

c) Ann does (his / her / its) homework.

d) The bicycle is at (his / her / its) place in the backyard.

e) My mom and I are at (our / your / their) house.

f) You wear (our / your / their) cap everywhere.

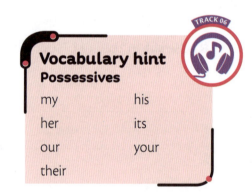

Vocabulary hint
Possessives
my   his
her   its
our   your
their

TRACK 06

3 Write the correct possessive adjective to each person bellow.

a) the boy _____

b) Maria _____

c) my cousins _____

d) the bird _____

e) my family and I _____

f) Philip and Elizabeth _____

g) I _____

h) you _____

28

Let's read n' write

1. Look at these movie posters and answer the questions.

GLOSSARY

Bigfoot: pé grande.

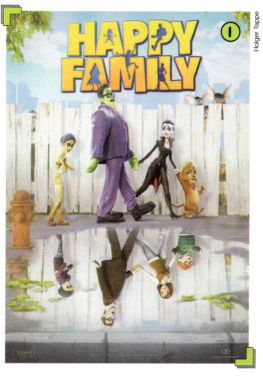

a) What are the movies about?

- ◯ Fashion.   • ◯ Families.   • ◯ Robots.   • ◯ Sports.

b) Circle all the elements that support your previous answer.

c) Where are they? Check where each movie seems to take place.

- Happy family.
  ◯ City.   ◯ Forest.

- The son of big foot.
  ◯ City.   ◯ Forest.

d) Mark with an **X** the elements that support your previous answer.

e) What elements support your answer?

- ◯ Images.   • ◯ Text.

f) What is their movie genre?

- ◯ Action.   • ◯ Animation.   • ◯ Drama.
- ◯ Adventure.   • ◯ Comedy.   • ◯ Horror.

29

g) Which is your favorite movie genre?

_____

h) What kind of information do these movie posters show? Check all possibilities.

- ( ) Director.
- ( ) Release date.
- ( ) Title.
- ( ) Place – where the story happens.
- ( ) Cast.
- ( ) Genre.

2 Write down the characters' family relationships.

a) *Happy family*

Emma   Frank   Fay   Max

_____   _____   _____   _____

b) *The son of Bigfoot*

Bigfoot   Adam   Shelly

_____   _____   _____

3 What are the special characteristics from the members of these families?

_____
_____
_____

4 Can you guess what the stories of the movies are?

_____
_____
_____
_____

5 Let's make a movie poster! Pair up and follow the instructions.

I. Your movie needs to have the following details:
- it is an animation.
- it is about a family with special / different characteristics.

II. You need to think about and decide.

a) What special characteristic does this family have?

_____

b) Where does the story take place?

_____

> **EXPLORING**
> - *Song of the sea*, 2014.
> - *Kung Fu Panda* 3, 2016.
> - *Storks*, 2016.
> - *The jungle book*, 2016.
> - *Despicable me* 3, 2017.
> - *The boss baby*, 2017.
> - *Coco*, 2017.

III. Think about your poster and all the elements it has.

What is the movie title?	
What is the movie genre?	
Who is the movie cast?	
What is the image of the poster?	
When is the release date?	

IV. Let's get to work! Use this space to make your movie poster using all the elements and ideas from the previous exercise.

CHAPTER 4

||| Citizenship moment |||

FAMILY RULES
Be Respectful and compassionate
Be HONEST and TRUSTWORTHY
Be RESPONSIBLE and ACCOUNTABLE
BE KIND AND HELPFUL TO OTHERS
CLEAN UP YOUR OWN MESS
Show respect for people's property
Do not argue or talk back in a disrespectful way
ASK PERMISSION
Share household chores
Keep your promises
HELP EACH OTHER
Say "i love you"
Always do your best
SAY "PLEASE", "THANK YOU" AND "EXCUSE ME"
ALWAYS TELL THE TRUTH
SHARE
LISTEN TO OTHERS
SHOW GRATITUDE

Kau Bispo

Based on the articles: <www.linkedin.com/pulse/top-10-family-rules-lahiri-shankar-achintya-lahiri> and <www.momjunction.com/articles/common-family-rules-parents-should-not-ignore_00346367/#gref>. Access: June 2018.

GLOSSARY

Accountable: responsável.
Argue (to argue): discuta (discutir).
Clean up (to clean up): limpe (limpar).
Compassionate: compassivo(a).
Do (to do): faça (fazer).
Help (to help): ajude (ajudar).
Helpful: útil.
Household chores: tarefas domésticas.
Keep (to keep): mantenha (manter).
Listen (to listen): ouça (ouvir).
Mess: bagunça.
Respectful: respeitoso(a).
Say (to say): diga, fale (dizer, falar).
Share (to share): divida (dividir).
Show (to show): demonstre (demonstrar).
Talk back (to talk back): responda, fale de volta (responder; falar de volta).
Tell (to tell): conte, fale (contar, falar).
Trustworthy: confiável.
Truth: verdade.

Let's practice

1 Check all the actions that illustrate the family rules presented.

2 Talk with your classmates.

a) What could you learn from these rules?
b) Why are they important to our lives?
c) How do they affect our environment?

PROJECT

Class rules

In groups, think about which rules could be established in the classroom to help build a good environment for everybody. Follow the teacher's instructions!

REVIEW

1) Choose the correct possessive adjective for the underlined word.

a) We have a <u>cat</u>. _____ name is Sunny.

b) <u>Mrs. O'Connel</u> has a van. _____ van is very old.

c) <u>We</u> go to secondary school. _____ school is fantastic.

d) <u>Mario</u> often visits _____ grandmother.

2) Complete using the affirmative form of verb to be (**am**, **is** or **are**).

a) Ann _____ my best friend.

b) Peter and Pamela _____ brother and sister.

c) Kevin _____ my cousin.

d) I _____ their classmate.

3) Rewrite the sentences from exercise 2 using the negative form.

a) _____

b) _____

c) _____

d) _____

4) Write the correct personal pronoun and correspondent possessive adjective to each image.

a)

b)

c)

d)

5. **Who are they? Write their family relationships.**

6. **Put the words in order and make interrogative sentences.**

   a) hungry / ? / you / are

   _____

   b) aunt / your / Laura / is / ?

   _____

   c) Monique / and / are / ? / Fred / relatives

   _____

   d) cat / is / Snowball / your / ?

   _____

7. **Match the sentences to the correct question word.**

   a) "_____ is your name?"
   "My name is Lisa."

   b) "_____ is your vacation?"
   "My vacation is in May."

   c) "_____ do you live?"
   "I live in Seattle."

   • What

   • Where

   • When

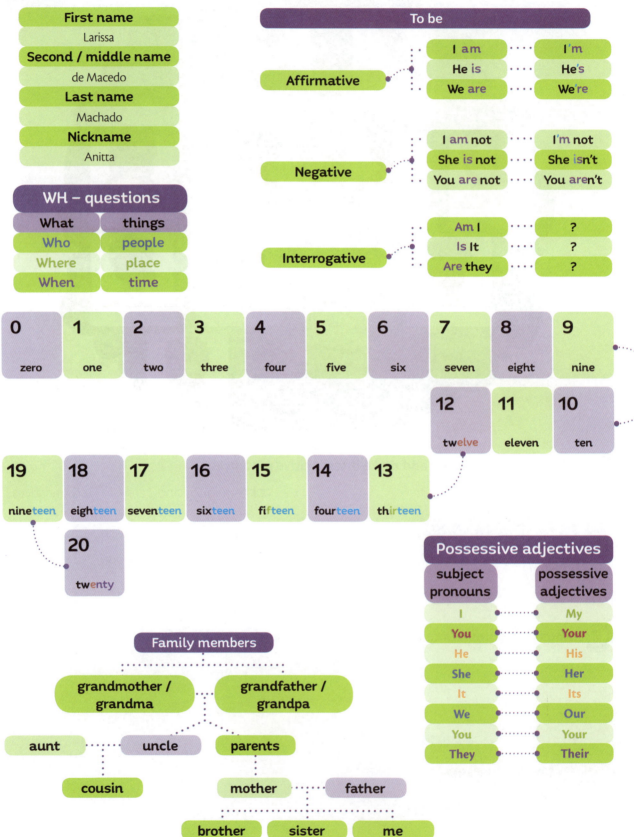

OVERCOMING CHALLENGES

(UERJ – 2017)

Na tirinha, Calvin e seu pai conversam sobre um assunto importante. Com base no primeiro quadrinho, indique o que motivou essa conversa. Identifique, ainda, os referentes do pronome **we** no primeiro e no último quadrinho, respectivamente.

GLOSSARY
Fun: divertido(a).
Report card: boletim.
To learn: aprender.
Written: escrito.

_____

_____

_____

_____

UNIT 3
HOW IS YOUR ROUTINE?

||| Get ready |||

1) Look at the comic strip. Who are the characters and what are their jobs?
_____

2) How is Lila's routine on Mondays? Check all the possibilities.

a) ◯ To brush the teeth.   e) ◯ To go to work.

b) ◯ To take a shower.   f) ◯ To read.

c) ◯ To have breakfast.   g) ◯ To wake up / To get up.

d) ◯ To go to school.   h) ◯ To play.

3) Is Lila happy? Why or why not?
_____

4) Which of these activities do you do daily? Do you like doing them?
_____
_____

CHAPTER 1

Let's practice

1 What are your daily activites? Check all possibilities.

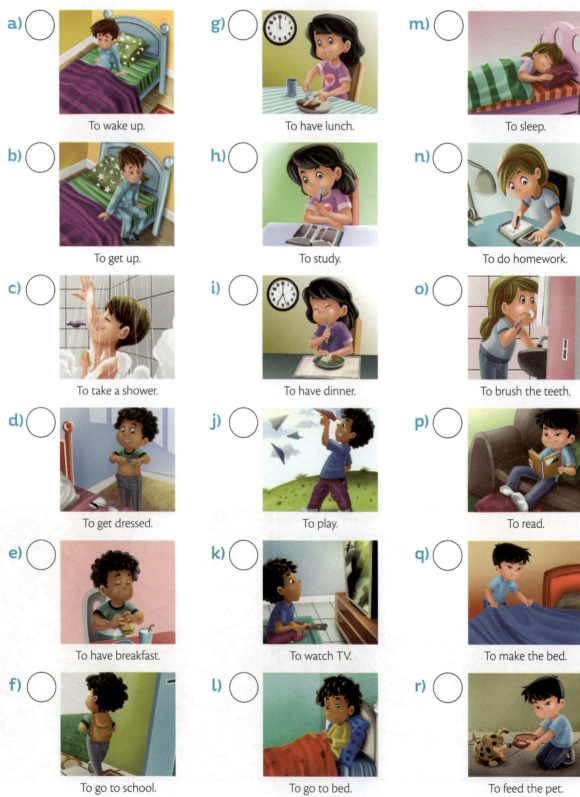

a) ◯ To wake up.
b) ◯ To get up.
c) ◯ To take a shower.
d) ◯ To get dressed.
e) ◯ To have breakfast.
f) ◯ To go to school.
g) ◯ To have lunch.
h) ◯ To study.
i) ◯ To have dinner.
j) ◯ To play.
k) ◯ To watch TV.
l) ◯ To go to bed.
m) ◯ To sleep.
n) ◯ To do homework.
o) ◯ To brush the teeth.
p) ◯ To read.
q) ◯ To make the bed.
r) ◯ To feed the pet.

2) **Look at the pictures and write the daily activity they represent.**

> To brush the teeth • To get dressed • To go to school
> To have lunch • To take a bath • To wake up

a)
_____

c)
_____

e)
_____

b)
_____

d)
_____

f)
_____

3) **Complete the sentences using the adverbs of frequency according to your habits.**

> always • usually • frequently • often • sometimes • rarely • hardly ever • never

a) I _____ eat bread at breakfast.

b) Mom and I _____ have lunch together.

c) I _____ do the homework.

d) I _____ feed my pet.

e) I _____ get up late.

f) I _____ brush my teeth after lunch.

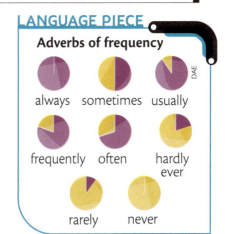

LANGUAGE PIECE
Adverbs of frequency

41

Let's listen n' speak

1 Listen to the article about daily routines.

Lifestyle

Why having a daily **routine** is important?

Developing a routine is a way of organizing your life into a coherent structure so that it makes sense to you and provides discipline in your life. It also **promotes** good **habits** and **increases** your efficiency, saving time in your **decision-making**.

To do something on an everyday basis, even if it is just **a little bit**, builds **strength** in the **long run**. It helps you **become** more proficient and **master** any skill; it will help you become more **adept** at what you do each day.

GLOSSARY

A little bit: um pouco.
Adept: conhecedor(a).
Become: tornar-se (tornar-se).
Decision-making: tomada de decisão.
Habits: hábitos.
Increases (to increase): aumenta (aumentar).
Long run: longo prazo.
Master: controlar.
Promotes (to promote): promove (promover).
Routine: rotina.
Strenght: força, ânimo.

Based on the articles: *18 Reasons Why a Daily Routine is so Important*, available at: <www.skilledatlife.com/18-reasons-why-a-daily-routine-is-so-important/>, *The Importance and benefits of keeping a Routine*, available at: <www.forbesfone.com/the-importance-and-benefits-of-keeping-a-routine>; and *Why having a Daily Routine Is Important*, available at: <https://examinedexistence.com/why-having-a-daily-routine-is-important/>. Access: Aug. 2018.

Now, check all the reasons why it is important to have a daily routine.

a) ◯ Organize life.
b) ◯ Build good habits.
c) ◯ Decrease efficiency.
d) ◯ Help to become good at things.
e) ◯ Build momentum in a short time.
f) ◯ Get you adept to daily activities.

2 Now, listen and read the article again. Use the following questions to talk to your classmates.

- Why is it important to be organized?
- How can a routine help you?
- How do you organize your daily activities?
- What good habits do you have in your routine? List all of them.

CHAPTER 2 — Let's practice

1 Complete with the affirmative form of the verbs in the present simple.

a) The kids _____ their pet. (to feed)

b) The boy _____ every morning. (to take a shower)

c) Babies _____ a lot. (to cry)

d) Luana _____ to pop music. (to listen)

> **LANGUAGE PIECE**
> **Present simple: affirmative form**
> Subject pronoun + **main verb** + **complement**.
> We **go** **to school in the morning**.

2 Put the following words in the correct order to form sentences in the affirmative.

a) pet / she / rarely / her / feeds

_____

b) goes to bed / my cousin / never / late

_____

c) by bus / usually / they / go to school

_____

d) dress up / by ourselves / for school / we / always

_____

> **LANGUAGE PIECE**
> **Present simple: affirmative form**
> 3rd person singular
> **verb** + (**-s**): eat**s**
> **verb** + (**-es**): watch**es**
> **verb** + (**-ies**): stud**ies**

3 Write the third person singular form of the following verbs.

a) believe _____

b) crash _____

c) do _____

d) drive _____

e) fix _____

f) match _____

g) think _____

h) wake _____

> **Vocabulary hint**
> **Verb ending in the Present simple**
> Add (-es) to verbs ending in:
> (-ch): watch – watches
> (-o): do – does
> (-sh): finish – finishes
> (-ss): pass – passes
> (-x): fix – fixes
> (-z): buzz – buzzes
>
> TRACK 08

4 Complete with the negative form of the present simple.

a) Kids _____ vegetables very much. (to like)

b) The boy _____ before lunch. (to take a shower)

c) The teachers _____ the homework. (to forget)

d) Mary _____ early on the weekends. (to wake up)

> **LANGUAGE PIECE**
>
> **Present simple: negative form**
> Subject pronoun + auxiliary verb + negative (not) + main verb + complement.
> We do not go to school in the morning.

5 Write the negative form of the verbs in the present simple.

a) I _____. (to do)

b) He _____. (to go)

c) We _____. (to sleep)

d) She _____. (to take)

e) They _____. (to have)

f) It _____. (to feed)

6 Complete the sentences with the best option.

a) _____ Mario _____ late on the weekends?
- ◯ Does / sleeps.
- ◯ Does / sleep.

b) _____ Anita _____ breakfast alone?
- ◯ Does / have.
- ◯ Do / has.

c) _____ the students _____ to school by bus?
- ◯ Does / go.
- ◯ Do / go.

d) _____ you _____ a lot?
- ◯ Do / studies.
- ◯ Do / study.

> **LANGUAGE PIECE**
>
> **Present simple: Interrogative form**
> Auxiliary verb + subject pronoun + main verb + complement?
> Do they go to school in the morning?

7 Mark if the sentence is **R** (right) or **W** (wrong).

a) ◯ Does Maria has lunch with her parents?

b) ◯ Do you do your homework everyday?

c) ◯ Does Joe get up early on the weekends?

d) ◯ Do they feeds their pets?

> **EXPLORING**
>
> Practice the *daily activities* vocabulary at:
> - https://learnenglishteens.britishcouncil.org/vocabulary/beginner-vocabulary/daily-routine

8. Use coins or pieces to represent each player in the board and roll the dice to choose who is going to play first. Each square has a task. Use present simple to answer the questions. The one who ends first wins the game.

Let's listen n' speak

1 Listen to the dialogue of Carl and Georgia and answer the questions.

a) What are they talking about? _____

b) What time does Georgia wake up? • ◯ 5 a.m. • ◯ 7 a.m.

c) Who wakes up early? • ◯ Carl. • ◯ Georgia.

d) When does Carl play soccer? • ◯ Monday. • ◯ Thursday.
 • ◯ Tuesday. • ◯ Friday.

e) What sport does Georgia play? • ◯ Football. • ◯ Volleyball. • ◯ Basketball.

2 Listen to the dialogue again and complete the sentences with the missing prepositions (**at**, **in**, **on**).

- Hey Carl, what is your morning routine?

- I wake up _____ 5 o'clock, take a shower and have breakfast, then I go to school. What about you?

- I wake up _____ 7 a.m., but only because I live close to school. Do you play soccer _____ Mondays?

- No, I don't. I play soccer _____ Thursdays. Do you play any sports?

- Yes, I do. I play volleyball _____ the park.

3 Complete the sentences with **at**, **in** or **on**.

a) My birthday is _____ September.

b) There are two books _____ the floor.

c) Vivian goes to the library _____ the afternoon.

d) The workers arrive _____ 9 a.m. _____ work.

Let's read n' write

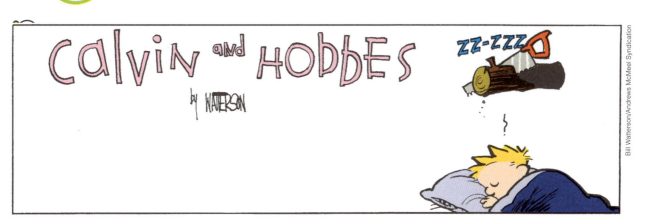

> **GLOSSARY**
>
> **Be late (to be late):** atrasar.
>
> **C'mon:** vamos lá.
>
> **Dreams:** sonhos.
>
> **Literal:** literal, ao pé da letra.
>
> **To wake up:** acordar.
>
> **Way too:** muito.

47

Let's practice

1) Observe Calvin and Hobbes comic strip and decide if the statements are **T** (true) or **F** (false).

a) ◯ Calvin wakes up and follows his daily routine to go to school.

b) ◯ Calvin dreams of waking up and following his daily routine to go to school.

c) ◯ Calvin's father wakes him up.

d) ◯ Calvin's mother wakes him up.

2) Why is Calvin annoyed?

a) ◯ Because he has to go to school.   b) ◯ Because his dreams are getting too literal.

3) What is Calvin's dream about?

_____

4) According to the comic strip, which activities does Calvin usually do before going to school? Check all the possibilities.

a) ◯   d) ◯   g) ◯

b) ◯   e) ◯   h) ◯

c) ◯   f) ◯   i) ◯

Ilustrações: Kau Bispo

5) Check the alternatives you identify yourself with.

a) ◯ I always have real dreams.

b) ◯ I hardly ever have dreams.

c) ◯ I usually dream about dragons and monsters.

48

d) ◯ I'm frequently afraid of what I'm dreaming.

e) ◯ Sometimes I have nightmares.

f) ◯ My dreams are never very fantastic.

g) ◯ In my dreams I can't see people's faces.

h) ◯ I often have dreams including my family.

i) ◯ Somebody told me that sometimes I speak when I'm dreaming.

> **EXPLORING**
> - *On my way to school*, by Sarah Maizes and Michael Paraskevas. Walker Childrens.
>
> **EXPLORING**
> - https://learnenglishkids.britishcouncil.org/en/category/topics/daily-routines

6 **What kind of text is a comic strip?**

a) ◯ A sequence of drawings, usually with dialogues representing a fun situation. It is telling a story or a joke.

b) ◯ A sequence of drawings, usually with no text representing a sad situation. It is telling a story or a joke.

7 **Discuss in small groups.**

a) How are the characters speeches presented?
- ◯ Speech bubbles.
- ◯ Narrator bubbles.
- ◯ Thought bubbles.
- ◯ Onomatopeia bubbles.

b) How are Calvin's actions shown?
- ◯ By drawings.
- ◯ By texts.
- ◯ By dialogues.
- ◯ By onomatopoeia.

c) What is the fun element in Calvin's story?

_____

8 **What about creating your own comic strip on your notebook? Follow the instructions and have fun!**

In pairs:
- brainstorm a daily routine theme for the comic strip;
- brainstorm a fun element related to the daily routine theme;
- brainstorm the events of the story.

On your own:
- think about the dialogues or onomatopoeias for the comic strip;
- detail the drawings and all the other elements that each scene should have.

CHAPTER 4

||| Citizenship moment |||

WHAT IS RESPONSIBILITY?

Being responsible **means** you do the things you are **expected** to do and **accept** the consequences (results) of your actions.

WHAT IS "A RESPONSIBILITY"?

A **responsibility** is something you are expected to do, like a **task** such as feeding your pet, or doing your homework.

WHAT IS "A CONSEQUENCE"?

A consequence is the result or **outcome** of our actions. Consequences can be positive (good) or negative (not good).

WHY IS IT IMPORTANT TO BE RESPONSIBLE?

When you are responsible, you have a positive outcome and you get the positive consequence for a job well done. If you are irresponsible, you **feel** the **pain** of a negative consequence for a job done **poorly** or **not at all**.

Being responsible **leads** to more trust and **freedom** because people know they can **count** on you to do the things you are expected to do. Being responsible can also be a big part of **keeping you safe**.

GLOSSARY

Accept (to accept): aceita (aceitar).
Count (to count): contar.
Expected: esperado(a).
Feel (to feel): sente (sentir).
Freedom: liberdade.
Keeping you safe: manter-se seguro(a).
Leads (to lead): conduz (conduzir).
Means (to mean): significa (significar).
Not at all: de modo algum.
Outcome: resultado.
Pain: dor.
Poorly: pobremente.
Responsibility: responsabilidade.
Task: tarefa.

Based on: *Talking with trees*: What is responsibility. Available at: <http://talkingtreebooks.com/definition/what-is-responsibility.htm>; *Kid's Health*: Rights and Responsibilities for Children. Available at: <http://www.cyh.com/HealthTopics/HealthTopicDetailsKids.aspx?p=335&np=287&id=1712>. Access: June 2018.

Let's practice

1 According to the text, what's the meaning of "to be responsible"? It means…

a) ◯ to do the opposite of what you are supposed to and to avoid the consequences.

b) ◯ to do things you are supposed to and to accept the consequences.

2 What are the text examples of responsibility? Can you think of other examples?

_____

_____

3 Say if the consequences are **P** (positive) or **N** (negative).

a) ◯ Sara is going to the school field trip because she did her homework and studied hard for her tests.

b) ◯ Mathew is going to buy a new bicycle because he helped with the house chores and saved his allowance.

c) ◯ Karen is not going to her friend's birthday party because she didn't finish her homework nor cleaned up her room.

d) ◯ Paul's parents are giving him a pet as a birthday gift because he proved to be responsible with all his chores.

e) ◯ The principal is with Aline's cell phone because she disobeyed the school rules and used it during the class.

f) ◯ Sebastian cannot go to his cousin's house this holiday because he is grounded for lying to his parents about his school grades.

EXPLORING

- *I Just Forgot*, by Mercer Mayer. Random House.
- *Arthur's Pet Business*, by Marc Brown. HachetteBook Group.
- *The Paperboy*, by Dav Pilkey. Orchard Books; Reissue edition.

PROJECT

Responsibility Chart
Team up and discuss with your classmates how can you be more responsible at home and at school. Think about the possible positive outcomes for each option.

4 Check all the options why being responsible is important.

a) ◯ negative outcome / consequence

b) ◯ positive outcome / consequence

c) ◯ leads to more trust and freedom

d) ◯ leads to less trust and freedom

e) ◯ people know they cannot count on you

f) ◯ people know they can count on you

g) ◯ keeps you safe

h) ◯ puts you in trouble

||| Get ready |||

1 Who are they?

Chaves • Madeline • Mickey Mouse • Mônica • Naruto • Peter Pan

I) _____   IV) _____

II) _____   V) _____

III) _____ VI) _____

2 Look at the flags. Which nationalities do they belong to?

Brazil • United Kingdom • France • Japan
Mexico • The United States of America – USA

I) _____   IV) _____

II) _____   V) _____

III) _____ VI) _____

Let's practice

1 Look at the flags and unscramble the letters to find out to which countries they belong.

a)
YTAIL

_____

b)
NASPI

_____

c)
LPTROUGA

_____

d)
RASTUALIA

_____

e)
YGNEARM

_____

f)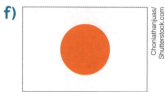
NAJPA

_____

g)
CINHA

_____

h)
MCEXOI

_____

i)
AGNTNRIAE

_____

j)
EPUR

_____

Let's listen n' speak

1 Listen the dialogue and organize the images in the correct order.

a) What are they talking about?

- ◯ Countries.
- ◯ Cities.
- ◯ Monuments.

b) What landmark are they building? Match.

- Bryana
- Alisha
- Lee
- Kiko

- Fontana di Trevi.
- Grand Canyon.
- Great Wall of China.
- Pyramid.

LANGUAGE PIECE

Question words

What asking for information about something.

c) What countries do they mention?

_____

_____

d) Check the countries where there are pyramids, according to the dialogue.

- ◯ China
- ◯ France
- ◯ Mexico
- ◯ Egypt
- ◯ Italy
- ◯ The USA

e) According to the dialogue, there are castles in _____

f) What monument is Lee building? Where is it from?

_____

g) What is Kiko doing?

- ◯ A sandcastle.
- ◯ A hole for his bone.
- ◯ A wall.

2 Where are these monuments from? Listen to the dialogue again and tell where each of the following monuments are from.

a)
Fontana di Trevi.
_____

c)
Great Wall of China.
_____

b)
Maya pyramid, Teotihuacan.
_____

d)
The Grand Canyon.
_____

3 In pairs, ask and answer questions using **what** and **where**.

- What is your nationality? *I am Brazilian.*
- Where would you like to go on your vacations? *I would like to go to The Grand Canyon.*
- Where is your favorite monument in the world? *My favorite monument is…*
- What country would you like to visit? *I would like to visit…*

LANGUAGE PIECE

Question words

Where asking about a place or position.

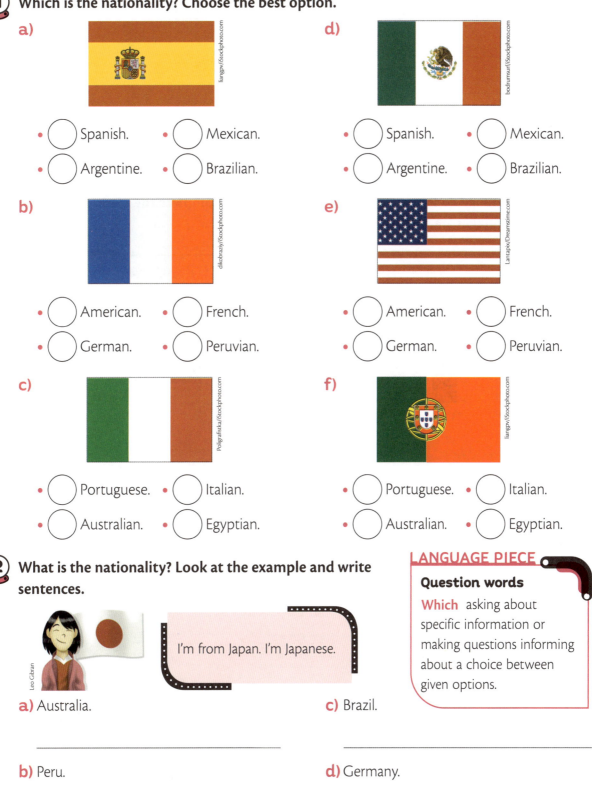

3) **Complete the sentences using what, which or where.**

a) _____ country has pyramids: Mexico or The USA?

b) _____ is your favorite monument in Brazil?

c) _____ are they from?

d) _____ country's flag do you like more?

e) _____ do you usually go on vacation?

f) _____ language do people speak in China?

4) **What language do they speak? Look the options and complete the cards. Pay attention, some languages are spoken in more than one place.**

Spanish • Italian • French • English • Portuguese
Japanese • Arabic • Chinese • German

Let's listen n' speak

1 Listen and complete the sentences. Use the words in the box.

> Germany's • Egypt's • Italy's • Japan's • Mary's
> Australia's • Spain's • Peru's • world's

a) _____ new hat is from France.

b) *Jámon serrano* is a typical _____ food.

c) _____ most famous animal is the kangaroo.

d) _____ capital is Berlin.

e) Burj Khalifa, in Dubai, is the _____ tallest building.

f) Shinkansen is _____ fastest train.

g) _____ capital, Lima, is one of the largest cities in South America.

h) _____ first pyramid was The Step Pyramid of Djoser.

i) Pizza is a traditional _____ foods.

LANGUAGE PIECE

Possessive case
Indicates possession.
Singular nouns add only (**-s**): mother's house.
Plural nouns ending in (**-s**) add only the apostrophe: sisters' house.

2 Rewrite the expressions using the possessive case.

a) the father of my friend _____

b) the teacher of my sister _____

c) the cellphone of Louis _____

3 Now it's your turn. Follow the instructions:

> Work in pairs. Your classmate has to make a sentence using the genitive case to describe the objects you point out. Each right sentence scores a point. The one with more points wins the game.

① **Rewrite the sentences using the genitive case.**

a) The house of Tony.
_____

b) The sons of Suzy.
_____

c) The father of Peter and Mary.
_____

d) The toys of the children.
_____

② **Complete the sentence using the given information.**

a) Bernard goes to a _____ after school. (house / friend)

b) She left the menu with the _____. (waiter / restaurant)

c) The soccer player doesn't go to the _____. (capital / country)

d) Cindy ride a bike at _____. (bikeway / city)

Vocabulary hint

Michael's cellphone
Mick and Charlie's
Parents' house
Paris' tower (or Paris's tower)
Week's news

③ **Read the sentences and write C (correct) or W (wrong) and rewrite the wrong ones.**

a) ( ) worke'r car _____

b) ( ) teacher's class _____

c) ( ) women's day _____

d) ( ) Peter' wallet _____

LANGUAGE PIECE

**Numbers:
ordinal x cardinal**

Cardinal numbers are used for counting.

Ordinal numbers are used for putting things in a sequence.

④ **Write the numbers in full.**

a) 1st _____

b) 2 _____

c) 5th _____

d) 8 _____

e) 2nd _____

f) 10 _____

g) 4th _____

h) 6 _____

Let's read n' write

1) Do you know New Zealand? Read its *Country facts form* and answer the questions.

\multicolumn{3}{c	}{**Country facts form – New Zealand**}
Name	New Zealand Aotearoa (Māori)	🇳🇿
Capital	Wellington	
Continent	◯ North America ◯ South America ◯ Europe ◯ Africa ◯ Antarctica ◯ Asia ◯ Australia / Oceania	(map of New Zealand)
Language	\multicolumn{2}{c	}{English (96.1%) Māori (3.7%) NZ Sign (0.5%)}
Climate	\multicolumn{2}{c	}{Temperature: four **distinct seasons**.}
Currency	\multicolumn{2}{c	}{New Zealand dollar}
Famous landmarks	\multicolumn{2}{c	}{Sky tower – **Tallest building** in New Zealand. Moeraki Boulders – Perfect **spherical rock** formations. Aoraki / Mount Cook – **Tallest mountain** in New Zealand.}

a) Which is the main language in New Zealand?

- ◯ NZ Sign.
- ◯ English.
- ◯ Māori.

b) What is New Zeland's name in Māori language?

_____

c) What is this landmark's name?

- Spherical Rock Formations.
- Tallest Mountain.
- Tallest Building.
- Sky tower.
- Moeraki Boulders.
- Aoraki.

d) What is New Zealand's currency?

- ◯ New Zealand real.
- ◯ New Zealand dollar.
- ◯ New Zealander.

GLOSSARY

Building: prédio.
Currency: moeda.
Distinct: distinto(a).
Landmark: marco.
Mountain: montanha.
Rock: pedra.
Seasons: estações do ano.
Spherical: esférico(a).
Tallest: mais alto(a).

61

e) How is the climate in New Zealand?

- ◯ The seasons are very similar.
- ◯ The seasons are very different.

f) Look at the map and locate where New Zealand is.

2 Let's analize the *Country facts form*.

a) What is this form about?

_____

b) What kind of information does it show?

- ◯ Capital city.
- ◯ Country's map.
- ◯ Landmarks.
- ◯ Total area.
- ◯ Religion.
- ◯ Natural resources.
- ◯ Climate.
- ◯ Country's name.
- ◯ Flag.
- ◯ Continent.
- ◯ Currency.
- ◯ Government.
- ◯ Time zone.
- ◯ Population.
- ◯ Language.

c) What other information do you think this kind of form should show?

_____

Let's make a *Country facts form*. Research and fulfill them.

a) Brazil

	Country facts form – Brazil	
Name		
Capital		
Continent	◯ North America ◯ South America ◯ Europe ◯ Africa ◯ Antarctica ◯ Asia ◯ Australia / Oceania	
Language		
Climate		
Currency		
Famous landmarks		

b) Choose a country you like.

	Country facts form	
Name		
Capital		
Continent	◯ North America ◯ South America ◯ Europe ◯ Africa ◯ Antarctica ◯ Asia ◯ Australia / Oceania	
Language		
Climate		
Currency		
Famous landmarks		

CHAPTER 4
||| Tying in |||

WORLD CONTINENTS

Here are some interesting facts about each of the continents that make them unique.

Antarctica
- Is the only continent completely **covered** in ice.
- Is the only continent that is **uninhabited** by humans (**although** some scientists **live** there for short periods of time).

Africa

- Has the second **largest** population in the world
- Contains the world's largest desert (The Sahara).
- Contains more countries than any other continent.
- Most of the world's gold and diamonds come from Africa.

Europe
- Through colonization, at one time **ruled** almost all of the rest of the world.
- Has been the starting point of **both** World Wars.

Asia
- Is the only continent joined to two others.
- Contains the top four most **populous** cities in the world.
- Contains the **highest** point on Earth (Mount Everest).
- Is the only continent where tigers are found in the **wild**.

Oceania

- Contains the **smallest** country by land area and population in the world (Nauru).
- Has more sheeps than people.
- Is the only continent that **lies** entirely in the **Southern** and **Eastern** Hemispheres.

GLOSSARY
Although: embora.
Both: ambos(as).
Covered: coberto.
Eastern: oriental, nativo do oriente.
Highest: o(a) mais alto(a).
Joined (to join): ligado(a) (ligar).
Largest: o(a) mais largo(a).
Lies (to lie): repousa (repousar).
Live (to live): vive (viver).
Northern: nativo do norte.
Populous: populoso(a).
Ruled (to rule): governado(a) (governar).
Smallest: o(a) menor.
Southern: do sul.
Southernmost: mais ao sul.
Tallest: o(a) mais alto(a).
Uninhabited: desabitado.
Western: ocidental, nativo do ocidente.
Wild: selvagem.

North America
- Is **joined** to Asia by ice in winter (Bering Sea).
- Is the only continent that lies entirely in the **Northern** and **Western** Hemispheres.
- Contains the world's **tallest** mountain (Mount Kea).
- Contains the world's largest fresh water lake (Lake Superior).

South America
- Contains the world's **southernmost** city (Punta Arenas).
- Contains the world's largest river system (The Amazon).

Based on: <www.kids-world-travel-guide.com/continent-facts.html> and <www.whatarethe7continents.com>. Access: June 2018.

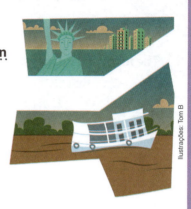

Let's practice

1) Read the following statements and decide if they are T (true) or F (false) according to the text.

a) ( ) Africa has the world's largest population.

b) ( ) Antarctica is the only continent uninhabited by the human beings.

c) ( ) Mount Everest is the highest point on Earth.

d) ( ) World War I and World War II began in Europe.

e) ( ) The smallest mountain in the world is located in North America.

f) ( ) Oceania has the biggest country in the world.

2) Answer the following statements based on the text.

a) Where is the Bering Sea?

_____

b) Where is the world's southernmost city?

_____

c) Where is the smallest country in the world?

_____

3) In your opinion, what was the most interesting curiosity about the continents and why?

PROJECT
My country's curiosities
Team up and choose a Brazilian region to research about it. Look for curiosities and unique traits of this region and make a chart showing your findings.

 EXPLORING

Geography games at the National Geographic Kids
- http://kids.nationalgeographic.com/kids/games/geographygames/

REVIEW

1) The following images show Clark's daily routine. Check five activities that are part of his routine.

a) ◯ wake up
b) ◯ drive
c) ◯ play video games
d) ◯ take a shower
e) ◯ have breakfast

f) ◯ watch TV
g) ◯ play basketball
h) ◯ make the bed
i) ◯ feed the pet
j) ◯ read

2) Use the present simple of the verbs in the indicated form.

a) Paul _____ a bike every day. (to ride – affirmative)

b) Pedro and John _____ soccer every day. (to play – negative)

c) The dog _____ every day. (to bark – affirmative)

d) The students _____ sciences every Friday. (to study – negative)

3) Rewrite the sentences from exercise 2 using the interrogative form.

a) _____

b) _____

c) _____

d) _____

4) Complete with the correct form of the genitive case.

a) the kid_____ toys
b) Oliver_____ car
c) Yesterday_____ dinner

d) the kids_____ toys
e) Lucas_____ pet
f) the girls_____ pens

5 Complete the table with the corresponding nationalities.

Flag	Country	Nationality
	Australia	
	The United States	
	Italy	
	Portugal	
	China	
	France	
	Brazil	
	Japan	

6 Complete the sentences with **Where**, **What**, or **Which**.

a) _____ does Paul ride a bike every week?

b) _____ does Paul ride at the park every week?

c) _____ place does Paul go to every week: the park or the gym?

7 Rewrite the sentences using the adverbs of frequency.

a) Peter plays volleyball. (usually) _____

b) We work on Mondays. (always) _____

c) I go to school on Sundays. (never) _____

d) Harry study hard. (sometimes) _____

DO NOT FORGET!

more frequent •─────────────────────────────• less frequent

always　　usually　　frequently　　often　　sometimes　　rarely　　hardly ever　　never

Present simple

Affirmative	He / She / It lives in Cuiabá.	I / You / We / They live in Macapá.
Negative	He / She / It does not live in Cuiabá.	I / You / We / They do not live in Macapá.
Interrogative	Does he /she / it live in Cuiabá?	Do you / we / they live in Macapá?

WH – questions
- What •······• things
- Where •······• places
- Which •······• options

Countries	Nationalities	Language
Brazil	Brazilian	Portuguese
The United States	American	English
Spain	Spanish	Spanish
Italy	Italian	Italian
France	French	French

- AT •······• clock time
- IN •······• longer periods
- ON •······• specific date

Genitive case
- Elizabeth's homework.
- The Smiths' house
- The children's toys.

ordinal numbers: 1st, 2nd, 3rd, 4th, 5th

Daily routine
- to get up
- to take a shower / to take a bath
- to have breakfast
- to read
- to have dinner
- to go to bed

68

OVERCOMING CHALLENGES

(VUNESP – 2013)

Leia a tirinha para responder à questão a seguir.

GLOSSARY

Beer: cerveja.
Breath: hálito.
Drinking (to drink): beber.
Eating (to eat): comer.
On the way: a caminho.
Sick and tired (expression): cansado, farto, sem disposição.
Smelling (to smell): sentir o cheiro, cheirar (cheirar).
To start: começar, iniciar.
To stop: parar.

No trecho do primeiro quadrinho – *she's sick and tired of smelling beer,* - **'s** pode ser reescrito como

a) is.

b) was.

c) goes.

d) does.

e) has.

(PUC-PR – 2006)

When Carlos has a headache, he _____ some tea.

a) is drinking

b) drank

c) used to drink

d) drinks

e) would drink

UNIT 5
WHAT ARE YOU DOING?

||| Get ready |||

1 What are they doing? Write the correct actions under the images.

reading • fishing • cooking • playing chess • acting • riding a bike

2 What kind of activities are they doing?

a) ◯ Free time / leisure activities.

b) ◯ Jobs.

c) ◯ Chores.

3 Do you do any of these activities? If not, which one would you like to do?

_____

_____

4 What else do you like to do in your free time?

_____

_____

Let's practice

1 What are they doing? Unscramble the letters and find out.

a)

G K S A I N T

She is roller _____.

b)

S I W M I N G M

He is _____.

c)

G A W I N T H C

She is _____ TV.

d)

P I G L A Y N

They are _____ video game.

e)

N I G N S I L E T

He is _____ to music.

f)

P I N A G T I N

She is _____.

2 Where do you do these activities? Label them O (outdoors) or I (indoors).

a) reading _____

b) fishing _____

c) cooking _____

d) playing chess _____

e) acting _____

f) riding a bike _____

g) roller-skating _____

h) swimming _____

i) watching TV _____

j) playing video game _____

k) listening to music _____

l) painting _____

3 Find six free time activities in the word search and make a sentence using each of them.

A	S	D	F	G	H	J	K	L	Q	W	E	R	T	P
Y	A	M	C	O	O	K	I	N	G	K	J	S	H	A
U	C	G	F	D	S	A	P	O	I	U	Y	W	P	I
I	T	T	R	E	W	Q	Z	X	C	V	B	I	L	N
O	I	A	S	F	I	S	H	I	N	G	G	M	M	T
P	N	P	O	I	U	Y	T	R	E	W	Q	M	O	I
Z	G	A	P	R	E	A	D	I	N	G	U	I	K	N
X	E	Q	Z	X	B	I	Z	Q	Z	Q	I	N	N	G
C	A	G	H	J	I	N	G	A	P	P	O	G	I	F

_____

_____

_____

_____

_____

_____

TRACK 13

1 Listen to the dialogue and answer the questions.

a) What each of them is doing?

- Tracy.

- John.

_____   _____

73

b) Say if it is **T** (true) or **F** (false).

- ( ) John does not want to play sports today.
- ( ) Somebody could play sports with John today.
- ( ) Tracy is good at doing archery.
- ( ) Tracy invites John to go cycling.

c) What about you? What do you enjoy doing in your free time?

_____

_____

2 Look at John's speech and tell if we use **do**, **play** or **go** with these activities.

> "I like to **play** soccer, **go** cycling and **do** archery."

a) _____ gymnastics

b) _____ basketball

c) _____ roller-skating

d) _____ ballet

e) _____ chess

f) _____ fishing

LANGUAGE PIECE

Play x Go x Do

Play sports with a ball or recreational games.

Do recreational games, physical activities, and martial arts.

Go sports ending with (**-ing**).

3 In pairs, complete the box with the correct verb to each activity. Then, mimic one of them and let your partner guess what it is. Follow the example.

_____ karate	_____ cycling	_____ gymnastics
_____ board games	_____ table tennis	_____ volleyball
_____ tennis	_____ judo	_____ badminton
_____ cards	_____ swimming	_____ running
_____ surfing	_____ yoga	_____ soccer

A: You're doing yoga.

B: No, I'm not. / No, you're wrong.

B: You're playing cards.

A: Yes, I am. / Yes, you're right.

CHAPTER 2

Let's practice

1 Put the following verbs in the affirmative form of present continuous. Follow the example.

> I – to do: I am doing.

a) You – to dance _____

b) He – to go _____

c) She – to paint _____

d) It – to eat _____

e) We – to watch _____

f) They – to fish _____

> **LANGUAGE PIECE**
>
> **Present continuous – affirmative form**
>
> Subject pronoun + auxiliary verb (*to be*) + main verb (+ *-ing*) + complement.
>
> You are reading my favorite book.

2 What are they doing? Write sentences using the present continuous.

a)

_____

c)

_____

b)

_____

d)

_____

Ilustrações: Kau Bispo

TRACK 14

Vocabulary hint
/-ing/ sounds

In the present continuous the (*-ing*) is pronounced like "**in**", the final (*-g*) is not pronounced:

swimm**ing**   watch**ing**   do**ing**

75

e)  g)

_____ _____

f)  h)

_____ _____

3 Put the following sentences in the correct order to form negatives in the present continuous.

a) I / fishing / not / am

_____

b) You / not / soccer / playing / are

_____

c) not / She / painting / is

_____

d) TV / We / not / are / watching

_____

e) He / roller-skating / not / is

_____

f) video game / are / They / playing / not

_____

4 Complete the sentences using the negative form of the verbs in the present continuous.

a) I _____ in class. (to dance)

b) You _____ a bicycle now. (to ride)

c) He _____ dinner. (to cook)

d) She _____ a schoolbook. (to read)

e) We _____ chess. (to play)

f) They _____. (to swim)

LANGUAGE PIECE

Present continuous – negative form

Subject pronoun + auxiliary verb (*to be*) + not + main verb (+ *-ing*) + complement.

You are not reading my favorite book.

5) Answer the questions based on the images.

a)

Is he playing soccer?

_____

c)

Are they having dinner?

_____

b)

Is she doing yoga?

_____

d)

Is he relaxing?

_____

6) Rewrite the sentences in the question form.

a) I am playing chess at school.

_____

b) You are roller-skating on the street.

_____

c) He is cooking lunch.

_____

d) She is playing soccer.

_____

e) We are watching TV.

_____

f) They are reading a literature book.

_____

7) Make two questions in the present continuous using the verbs from the box.

to fish • to swim

LANGUAGE PIECE

Present continuous – interrogative form
Auxiliary verb (**to be**) + Subject pronoun + main verb (+ **-ing**) + complement.
Are you reading my favorite book?

_____

_____

_____

8) Interview a few friends and find out what they are doing. Use your notebook. Be creative.

Let's listen n' speak

1 Listen to four dialogues. Who is...

Carmen • Elsa • Jason • Jean • Marco • Noriko • Sylvia • Yolanda

a) ... watching a movie? _____.

b) ... doing yoga? _____.

c) ... listening to music? _____.

d) ... playing chess? _____.

2 Check only the true statements.

a) ◯ Jean is watching a movie.

b) ◯ Jean is studying math.

c) ◯ Yolanda is roller–skating in the park.

d) ◯ Yolanda's yoga class is beginning.

e) ◯ Noriko is watching a movie.

f) ◯ Elsa is listening to music.

g) ◯ Marco is roller-skating in the park.

h) ◯ Marco is playing chess with his dad.

3 Who wants to do this?

a)
_____

c)
_____

b)
_____

d)
_____

4 What are your classmates doing now? Pair up and talk about what you observe.

CHAPTER 3

Let's read n' write

1) What are you doing on your next summer vacations? Read the following pamphlet and answer the questions.

a) When is the Summer camp happening?

- ◯ 5/25 to 6/27
- ◯ 6/25 to 7/27
- ◯ 7/25 to 8/27

b) How much is it going to cost?

- ◯ US$ 10,000.
- ◯ US$ 20,000.
- ◯ US$ 50,000.

c) How many hours per day do the activities of the Summer camp take?

- ◯ 6 hours and a half.
- ◯ 7 hours and a half.
- ◯ 8 hours and a half.

d) What kind of activities are happening at the Summer camp? Check all possibilities.

- ◯ Practicing sports.
- ◯ Water activities.
- ◯ Equestrian activities.
- ◯ Culinary classes.
- ◯ Building a bonfire in the open space.
- ◯ Making crafts.
- ◯ Daily trips.
- ◯ Artistic activities.

e) Who can enroll in the Summer camp?

- ◯ Kids up to twelve years old.
- ◯ Kids from six to twelve years old.

f) Which class is optional?

- ◯ Equitation classes.
- ◯ Spanish classes.
- ◯ Culinary classes.

g) What are the means of contact?

- ◯ Telephone.
- ◯ Email.
- ◯ Visit.

h) What meals are included?

_____

2 Say if it is T (true) or F (false).

a) ◯ The camp is only for boys.
b) ◯ The camp takes place from Monday to Friday.
c) ◯ Kids who are 12 years old can go.
d) ◯ Two-day excursions are happening during the camp.
e) ◯ Handicraft activities are offered.
f) ◯ There are a good number of activities being offered.

3 Analyze the pamphlet.

a) What is the aim of this pamphlet?

- ◯ To announce an event.
- ◯ To sell a product.
- ◯ To offer a service.

b) Who is this pamphlet addressed to?

- ◯ Parents.
- ◯ Kids.
- ◯ Teachers.

c) What kind of text is used on the pamphlet? Check all possibilities.

- ◯ Descriptive.
- ◯ Informative.
- ◯ Narrative.
- ◯ Report.
- ◯ Explanatory.
- ◯ Instructive.
- ◯ Persuasive.
- ◯ Review.

d) What kind of information does the pamphlet present? Check all possibilities.

- ◯ Date and time.
- ◯ Professionals.
- ◯ Price.
- ◯ Activities.
- ◯ Audience.
- ◯ Telephone.
- ◯ Location.
- ◯ Photos.
- ◯ Organizer.

4 Let's make a Summer camp poster! Think about the following topics. Use your notebook to take notes.

a) What is the aim of this pamphlet?

b) Who is this pamphlet addressed to?
- Gender.
- Age group.

c) What is its title?

d) What kind of information does the pamphlet present?

e) What kind of activities are offered?

f) Where is it going to happen?

g) When is it going to happen?

h) What are the means of contact?

i) Who are the organizers?

j) How much does it cost?

k) What kind of images can be used?

5 Now, let's get down to work!

1. Write a draft of the phamplet using the information you selected.
2. Exchange it with a partner and correct one another's drafts.
3. Rewrite your draft with all the corrections.
4. Present the corrected pamphlet to your teacher.
5. Make a final version of it using your teacher's correction. Use images and different types of materials.

EXPLORING

- *Goodnight Campsite,* by Loretta Sponsler and Olga Shevchenko. CreateSpace Independent Publishing Platform.
- *Into the Outdoors,* by Susan Gal. Knopf Books for Young Readers.

EXPLORING

Nature games PBS Kids
- http://pbskids.org/games/nature/

Camp Wonderopolis
- https://camp.wonderopolis.org/

81

CHAPTER 4
||| Citizenship moment |||

SCOUTS

What is it?
The Scout Movement started in 1907, with 20 boys in an experimental camp organized by the Lieutenant-General Robert Baden-Powell. Nowadays, there are more than 40 million Scouts, young people and adults, male and female, in over 200 countries and territories.

GLOSSARY
- **Citizens:** cidadãos.
- **Courteous:** cortês.
- **Deed:** ato, feito.
- **Duty:** dever.
- **Growth:** crescimento.
- **Strengthening:** fortalecimento.
- **Thrifty:** econômico.
- **Whistles under all difficulties:** não se intimida.

How does it work?
It provides opportunities to participate in programs, events, activities and projects that contribute to youth's growth as active citizens.

What is its mission?
It is to contribute to the education of young people, to help build a better world.

What are its priorities?

YOUTH ENGAGEMENT
Empower the participants to take an active part in their communities.

EDUCATIONAL METHODS
A non-formal learning environment, strengthening the capacity of facing the challenges.

DIVERSITY & INCLUSION
It should reflect its societies and actively work to welcome all individuals without distinction.

SOCIAL IMPACT
Through activities and projects to contribute to the communities and become leaders of positive change.

The Scout Principles

Duty to God – a person's relationship with the spiritual values of life.

Duty to others – a person's relationship with, and responsibility within: family, local community, country and the world, as well as respect for others and for the natural world.

Duty to self – a person's responsibility to develop his or her own potential, to the best of that person's ability.

The Scout Law

1. A Scout's honour is to be trusted.
2. A Scout is loyal.
3. A Scout's duty is to be useful and to help others.
4. A Scout is a friend to all and a brother to every other Scout.
5. A Scout is courteous.
6. A Scout is a friend to animals.
7. A Scout obeys orders of his parents, Patrol Leader or Scoutmaster without question.
8. A Scout smiles and whistles under all difficulties.
9. A Scout is thrifty.
10. A Scout is clean in thought, word and deed.

Based on: *World Scouting*. Available at: <www.scout.org>; *Scouts*. Available at: <www.scouts.org.uk/home/>. Access: June 2018.

Let's practice

1 What are the scout priorities?

a) Social
b) Youth
c) Diversity
d) Educational

- Methods.
- Engagement.
- Impact.
- Inclusion.

2 What is the synonym?

a) Useful.
- ◯ Helpful.
- ◯ Intelligent.

b) Thrifty.
- ◯ Nice.
- ◯ Economic.

c) Actively.
- ◯ Destroy.
- ◯ Energetic.

d) Courteous.
- ◯ Respectful.
- ◯ Dirty.

PROJECT

Scouts

Research about the Scout's movement. Gather all the information you can and choose the three most interesting and relevant ones to present to your classmates.

EXPLORING

Top 6 Scouting Organizations for children
- www.thespruce.com/scouting-organizations-for-kids-2087396

Grupos de escoteiros
- www.escoteiros.org.br/grupos-escoteiros/

3 Read the text again and say to which Scout's Law it belongs.

a) ◯ A scout helps a bird to fly.
b) ◯ A scout helps a person to cross the street.
c) ◯ A scout spends $ 10 not $ 50.
d) ◯ A scout respects his parents.

4 What is this Scout's Principle?

duty to self • duty to God • duty to others

a) The relationship with yourself. _____

b) The relationship with and responsibility within everything and person in the surroundings.
_____

c) The relationship with spiritual values of life. _____

83

UNIT 6
WHAT TYPE OF HOUSE IS IT?

||| Get ready |||

1. What type of houses are these? Look at the images, talk with your teacher and classmates and write the correct name under the images.

> yurt • mud house • igloo • cave house
> brick house • stilt house

2. Do you know any of these types of houses?

_____
_____

3. Which one do you think is the most interesting? Why?

_____
_____
_____

Let's practice

1 What type of house is this? Look at the images, read the definitions and write the correct name to each of them.

_____   _____   _____

a) It is a boat that people use as home: _____.

b) It is a type of house that can be moved using a vehicle: _____.

c) It is a shelter made of cloth. Poles and ropes support it: _____.

d) It is a set of rooms for living in, especially on one floor of a building: _____.

e) It is a construction where one or more families can live: _____.

f) It is on a farm: _____.

2 What about you? Which of the following constructions do you know? Check all true options for you.

a) ◯ Boathouse.   e) ◯ House.   i) ◯ Igloo.

b) ◯ Mobile home / trailer. f) ◯ Farmhouse.   j) ◯ Mud house.

c) ◯ Tent.   g) ◯ Brick house.   k) ◯ Stilt house.

d) ◯ Flat / apartment.   h) ◯ Cave house.   l) ◯ Yurt.

3 Which parts of the house are these? Solve the codes and find out.

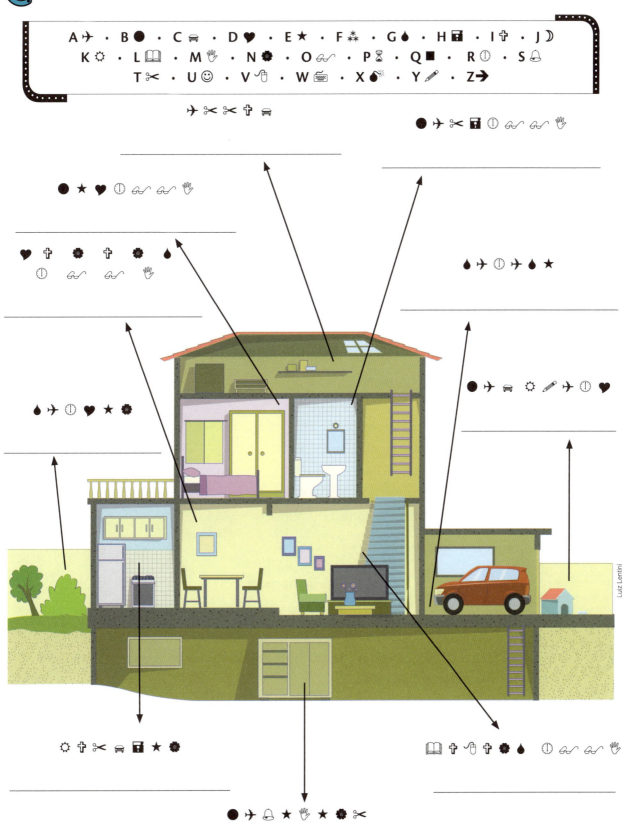

Let's listen n' speak

1 Listen to Karen talking about her grandparents' house and write T (true) or F (false).

a) ◯ Karen's grandparents live in a trailer.

b) ◯ Karen's grandparents live in the USA.

c) ◯ There is only one floor in the house.

d) ◯ There is an attic, a basement, a kitchen, and a bathroom.

e) ◯ There are two bedrooms and two bathrooms.

f) ◯ There is a beautiful and flowered garden.

g) ◯ There is no backyard.

2 Listen to the audio again and answer the following questions.

a) Where do the grandparents live?

_____

b) What type of house do the grandparents have?

_____

c) How many are there? Write the correct number.

- ◯ attic
- ◯ kitchen
- ◯ bathroom
- ◯ basement
- ◯ living room
- ◯ garden
- ◯ bedroom
- ◯ dining room
- ◯ backyard

3 Let's make a House Riddle? Look at the example and use your imagination to make a riddle about the parts of the house.

> **Living room**
> You can relax here. There is usually a sofa. I'm a room. People often watch TV here.

_____

_____

88

Let's practice

1 Can you match the object with its name?

microwave oven • sink • armchair • chair • couch • refrigerator
table • stove • bed • bathtub • toilet seat • bookshelf

a)
_____

b)
_____

c)
_____

d)
_____

e)
_____

f)
_____

g)
_____

h)
_____

i)
_____

j)
_____

k)
_____

l)
_____

Ilustrações: Marcelo Azalim

89

2 Now, organize the items from the previous exercise in the correct place.

kitchen	living room	dining room	bedroom	bathroom

3 Which is the correct option? Circle it.

a) _____ a lamp in the bedroom. (There is / There are)

b) _____ three glasses on the table. (There is / There are)

c) _____ two tables in the kitchen. (There is / There are)

d) _____ one person at the bus stop. (There is / There are)

e) _____ a little cat behind the tree. (There is / There are)

f) _____ lots of books on the shelf. (There is / There are)

LANGUAGE PIECE

There is x There are
Used to say that something exists or does not exist.
There is – singular.
There are – plural.

4 Pair up and talk about the following scene. What is / are there on the picture?

_____
_____
_____
_____
_____
_____
_____

5 Choose the best alternative to complete the sentences.

a) The mail is _____ the mailbox.
- ◯ on   • ◯ at   • ◯ in

b) My dog always sleeps _____ my bed.
- ◯ on   • ◯ at   • ◯ in

c) The plates are not _____ the table.
- ◯ on   • ◯ at   • ◯ in

d) Meg is _____ Glen's house.
- ◯ on   • ◯ at   • ◯ in

e) There is an ambulance _____ my house.
- ◯ on   • ◯ at   • ◯ in

f) There is a big wardrobe _____ my room.
- ◯ on   • ◯ at   • ◯ in

g) My mother works _____ a restaurant.
- ◯ on   • ◯ at   • ◯ in

h) There is a stain _____ the window glass.
- ◯ on   • ◯ at   • ◯ in

Vocabulary hint

Linking sounds

Coarticulation:

in an office

on a square bench.

Elision:

at the end

6 Complete the following sentences using **at, in** or **on**.

a) Jane is waiting _____ the bus stop.

b) He is standing _____ the street.

c) Do you work _____ an office?

d) Do you live _____ Japan?

e) There was a "no smoking" sign _____ the wall.

f) The shop is _____ the end of the street.

LANGUAGE PIECE

Prepositions of place
at x in x on

At – specific point or location.

In – enclosed space; inside something.

On – surface.

Let's listen n' speak

1 Listen to the audio, look at the photos and number them accordingly.

2 Listen again and check if the dialogues are **A** (affirmative) or **N** (negative).

a) ◯ one   **b)** ◯ two   **c)** ◯ three   **d)** ◯ four

3 Circle the correct option according to the sequence in the audio.

a) (There is / There are) a car, a motorcycle and a bicicle in the garage.

b) (There is / There are) not any pans on the stove.

c) (There is / There are) not any milk.

d) (There is / There are) one of them in the living room.

4 In pairs, talk about the image below.

A: Are there any stoves?
B: No, there aren't any stoves.
A: How many sofas are there?
B: There is one sofa.

Let's read n' write

1 Think about where you live and talk with your friends about the following topics.

a) Do you live in a house, in an apartment or in a different place?

b) Is it your own place or is it rented?

c) How can you find places for renting?

- ◯ Classified ads.
- ◯ TV programs.
- ◯ Books.

2 Read the following classified ad.

☆—— CLASSIFIED – REAL ESTATE ——☆

FOR RENT

Studio apart semi furnished for rent. $550 per month + $50. Dish, T.V., excluding water and light. Wi-Fi included. No kids, only permanente workers. Location: Lilidge Road, Madame Estate. Call: 588-1216.

Apartments for rent!
Staghorn Coral, Beacon Hill: 1 bedroom furnished, hot & cold, A/C, parking, $800 excluding utilities. No pets. Call: 523-9377.

Cole Bay: Almond Grove
With 24/7 security, nice 2 bedrooms, 1 bath, unfurnished with common pool (no view). $1,500 monthly. No pets. Call: 581-6418.

Cole Bay
For rent 4 bedrooms, 3 baths, beautiful view, sits on a hill, quiet area. $2,100 monthly, 2 months security deposit. Available now. Call: 555-7478.

★ **Cote d'Azur Marina** ★
Cupecoy: Waterfront, one bedroom apartment for rent. Fully furnished and equipped. Available July 1st. Rent $1,300 plus utilities. For more information call: 581-6545.

Mary's Fancy for rent
Hilltop. Brand new, 3 bedrooms, 2 baths, spacious home, garden, alarm, security, generator, cistern, concrete roof, and shutters. Call for viewing 580-2588.

★ **Guana Bay Villa** ★
3 bedrooms with A/C, 2 baths, plus 2 guestrooms with baths, large private garden, large terrace, ocean view, $2,500. Interested persons only. Call between 2 p.m. – 6 p.m., 522-5499, wilkoca@hotmail.com

Luxury
2 bedrooms apartment about 150m² in Philipsburg, sea view. Swimming pool, generator, elevator, parking, and internet included. Security guard, safe building. $2,500 p/m + fees. Call: 590-690 or charles.kimberley@hotmail.us

★★★★★★★★★★★

GLOSSARY

A/C: ar-condicionado.
Brand new: novo, sem uso anterior.
Furnished: mobiliado.
Parking: estacionamento.
Permanent workers: trabalhadores permanentes.
Plus: mais, em adição.
Quiet: calmo, silencioso.
Security deposit: depósito de segurança.
Shutters: persianas.
Unfurnished: não mobiliado.
Utilities: serviços.
Waterfront: beira-mar.

a) What newspaper's section are the classified ads published on?

_____

b) How many of them are there?

- Houses: _____
- Apartment: _____

c) How much does it cost per month to live at…

- … Lilidge Road, Madame Estate? _____
- … Staghorn Coral, Beacon Hill? _____
- … Cote d'Azur Marina? _____
- … Philipsburg? _____

d) Tell if the place is **F** (furnished) or **U** (unfurnished).

- ( ) Studio apartment.
- ( ) Apartments of rent.
- ( ) Cole Bay: Almond Grove.
- ( ) Cote d'Azur Marina.

e) Which place…

- … can be contacted by phone and email? _____.
- … does not allow pets? _____.
- … does not allow children? _____.
- … needs a security deposit? _____.
- … can be phoned only between 2 p.m. and 6 p.m.? _____.
- … includes Wi-Fi? _____.
- … includes A/C? _____.
- … has a waterfront? _____.
- … includes a pool? _____.
- … includes an elevator? _____.

3) Analyze the classified ad.

a) What is the purpose of classified ads?

- ( ) Build apartments.
- ( ) Rent apartments.
- ( ) Destroy apartments.

b) What characteristics are described in the ads?

- ( ) Number of rooms.
- ( ) Number of bathrooms.
- ( ) Furniture items.
- ( ) Region.
- ( ) Full address.
- ( ) Telephone and email.
- ( ) Size.
- ( ) Utilities.
- ( ) Condominium.
- ( ) Price.
- ( ) Housing type.
- ( ) Owner.

4 Let's make a classified ad. Pair up and decide on the following information.

a) What is it? A house, an apartment, a studio etc.? _____

b) How big is it? How many bedrooms and bathrooms? _____

c) Where is it? _____

d) What is included in the rent? _____

e) How much does it cost monthly? _____

f) What are the utilities available? _____

g) How can it be contacted? _____

5 Now, make your classified ad using all the elements and ideas you listed previously.

EXPLORING

- *Homes Around the World*, by Dona Herweck Rice. Teacher Created Materials.

EXPLORING

- *Up*, 2009.
- *Jumanji*, 2017.
- *Foster Home for Imaginary Friends*, 2004.

EXPLORING

Kids World Citizen
- https://kidworldcitizen.org/a-look-at-houses-around-the-world/

17 of the Most Amazing Treehouses From Around The World
- www.boredpanda.com/amazing-treehouses/

||| Tying in |||

Have you ever heard of EARTH HOUSES?

Lyfestyle

Earth Sheltered Homes

"Another type of building is emerging: one that actually heals the scars of its own construction. It conserves rainwater and fuel and it provides a habitat for creatures other than the human one. Maybe it will catch on, maybe it won't. We'll see." – Malcolm Wells, 2002.

Earth sheltered house in Zurich, Switzerland.

The earth sheltered home uses the ground as an insulating blanket, which effectively protects it from temperature extremes, wind, rain and extreme weather events. An earth sheltered home is energy-efficient, quiet, freeze-proof and low maintenance. Aesthetically an earth sheltered home blends in with the natural environment, leaving more yard space and more space for wildlife.

[...] Many earth homes incorporate passive solar designs, lessening even further the need for fuel for heating or cooling.

Earth sheltered house in Norway.

The 2 types of earth sheltered homes

Earth Sheltered: Dirt covers three exterior sides and the roof (the walls are most often concrete).

Earth Bermed: Dirt is pushed up against the exterior walls only, and not onto the roof, yet the roof is usually super-insulated. [...]

> **GLOSSARY**
>
> **Blanket:** cobertor.
> **Blends in (to blend in):** mistura-se (misturar-se).
> **Catch on (to catch on):** tornar-se popular.
> **Dirt:** terra.
> **Energy-efficient:** energeticamente eficiente.
> **Freeze-proof:** à prova de congelamento.
> **Fuel:** combustível.
> **Heal:** cura.
> **Lessening (to lessen):** diminuindo (diminuir).
> **Maintenance:** manutenção.
> **Onto:** em cima.
> **Pushed up (to push up):** impulsionada (impulsionar).
> **Scar:** cicatriz.

Insteading. Available at: <www.inspirationgreen.com/earth-sheltered-homes.html>. Access: June 2018.

Let's practice

1) What is an earth-sheltered home?

a) ◯ It uses the ground as an insulating blanket.

b) ◯ It doesn't protect from extreme temperatures.

c) ◯ It saves energy.

d) ◯ It has a high maintenance.

2) According to the text, what type of building is emerging?

_____

_____

3) Match the expressions from the text with their meanings.

a) insulating blanket

b) energy-efficient

c) freeze-proof

d) low maintenance

e) blends in with the natural environment

- ◯ protects from very cold temperatures
- ◯ it goes well with nature
- ◯ because it is underground, it keeps the temperature
- ◯ needs less energy than conventional houses
- ◯ it is easy to keep it in good conditions

EXPLORING

- *If you lived here: Houses of the World,* by Giles Laroche. HMH Books for Young Readers.
- *Sustainable Houses,* by Jacobo Krauel. Links International.

4) What could be done to have a comfortable and sustainable residence?

_____

_____

_____

_____

PROJECT

Sustainable materials

Choosing materials is an important part in building a sustainable home. In groups, look at the list below and choose three to research about their usage. Make a poster with the information you collected.

- glass
- reclaimed wood
- soils
- plastic
- rammed earth
- steel
- bricks, stones, and pavers
- tyres
- straw bales
- bamboo

97

REVIEW

1) Complete with present continuous in the affirmative form of the verbs.

a) The students _____ gymnastics on Friday. (to do)

b) I _____ my bicycle. (to ride)

c) We _____ pasta. (to eat)

d) Mrs. O'Connel _____ an old magazine. (to read)

e) Our parents _____ TV. (to watch)

f) You _____ tennis with your big sister. (to play)

2) Rewrite the sentences from exercise 1 using the negative form.

a) _____

b) _____

c) _____

d) _____

e) _____

f) _____

3) Put the words in order and form interrogative sentences.

a) they / bowling / are / right now?

_____

b) your dad / good at / cards / playing / is?

_____

c) judo / are / at the moment / you / doing?

_____

d) Kim / this month / and / horseback riding / are / you / going?

_____

4 Read the sentences and circle the correct verb to complete them.

a) Your sister is _____ archery. (playing / doing / going)

b) Look! Romero is _____ karate. (playing / doing / going)

c) You are _____ skating now. (playing / doing / going)

d) Jules and Pierre are _____ yoga at the moment. (playing / doing / going)

e) This computer is good at _____ chess. (playing / doing / going)

f) We are _____ exercises for our legs this morning. (playing / doing / going)

5 Add the words according to the category given by the first word.

a) There is a refrigerator, _____, and _____.

b) There are birds, _____, and _____.

c) There is an armchair, _____, and _____.

d) There is a car, _____, and _____.

e) There is a bed, _____, and _____.

f) There is a shower, _____, and _____.

6 Check the correct option.

a) ◯ There is a mirrors.
   ◯ There is a mirror.

b) ◯ There are some chair.
   ◯ There are some chairs.

c) ◯ There is a dresser.
   ◯ There is dresser.

d) ◯ There are a rug.
   ◯ There are some rugs.

7 Complete the sentences using **at**, **in**, **on** and the given word.

a) The old books are _____ the table.

b) The red car is _____ my house.

c) All my friends are _____ the kitchen.

d) Those nice photos are hung _____ the wall.

99

DO NOT FORGET!

Play	Go	Do
(sports with a ball)	(movement)	(physical activities)
Play	Go	Do
basketball	skating	karate
volleyball	surfing	judo
baseball	bowling	taekwondo
tennis	bicycling	yoga
golf	climbing	gymnastics
rugby	fishing	ballet
chess	dancing	classes
cards	running	archery
board games	walking	aerobics

Bedroom: sleep.

Bathroom: take a shower.

Living room: relax/watch TV.

kitchen: cook.

Garage: park the car.

Garden / yard: play and / or grow plants.

Dining room: eat.

There is	singular (one) or uncountable nouns
There are	with plural (two or more)
Some	plural or uncountable nouns – affirmative
Any	plural or uncountable nouns – negatives and questions

Prepositions of place

AT	To indicate presence or location at a point
IN	To indicate enclosed spaces, inside, inclusion within space, a place or limits
ON	To indicate surface, contact

Present Continuous

Affirmative	You	are	reading.
Negative	You	are	not (aren't) reading.
Interrogative	Are	you	reading?

Present Continuous (-ing)

read	+ (-ing)	read**ing**
take	consonant + -e	tak**ing**
lie	verb ending in "ie"	ly**ing**
put	verb ending in vowel + consonant	putt**ing**

(Mackenzie – 2000)

Em inglês, "Você está esperando alguma carta?" seria:

a) Have you been waiting for a chart?

b) Are you expecting a letter?

c) Are you attending any lecture?

d) Are you staying for a lecture?

e) Have you been hoping for a lecture?

(Centec – 2015)

1 Complete the sentence with the correct verb form:

> Hans _____ at the library, that's why he _____ with us right now.

a) is studying – can't be

b) is not studying – are

c) studies – were

d) studied – have been

e) study – used to be

2 Check the sequence that matches correctly the verb tenses with the following sentences:

I. I am writing an essay about global warming.

II. His father likes to watch football games.

III. He was a lovely grandfather.

a) Present Simple – Present Perfect – Present Continuous.

b) Present Continuous – Present Simple – Past Simple.

c) Present Continuous – Present Simple – Present Perfect.

d) Present Simple – Present Continuous – Present Perfect.

e) Present Perfect – Present Continuous – Past Simple.

UNIT 7
WHO ARE THEY?

Zootopia.

Sing.

Madagascar.

||| Get ready |||

1) Who are they? Check all possibilities.

a) ◯ Actors.   c) ◯ People.

b) ◯ Animals.   d) ◯ Characters.

2) Have you ever seen any of these animals? Where?

_____

_____

3) What are their names? Look at the images and check all you can see.

a) ◯ Squirrel.   j) ◯ Pig.   s) ◯ Toucan.

b) ◯ Raccoon.   k) ◯ Sloth.   t) ◯ Goat.

c) ◯ Hippopotamus.   l) ◯ Cow.   u) ◯ Rabbit.

d) ◯ Turtle.   m) ◯ Bull.   v) ◯ Fox.

e) ◯ Giraffe.   n) ◯ Mouse.   w) ◯ Gorilla.

f) ◯ Penguin.   o) ◯ Dog.   x) ◯ Sheep.

g) ◯ Elephant.   p) ◯ Koala.   y) ◯ Tiger.

h) ◯ Lemur.   q) ◯ Monkey.   z) ◯ Bison.

i) ◯ Zebra.   r) ◯ Hedgehog.

Ferdinand.

Let's practice

1) What animal is this? Look at the image and write its name.

zebra • rabbit • pig • monkey • lion • giraffe • ferret • dog • cow • chicken

a)
_____

b)
_____

c)
_____

d)
_____

e)
_____

f)
_____

g)
_____

h)
_____

i)
_____

j)
_____

Ilustrações: Luiz Lentini

Let's listen n' speak

1) There are many different animals in the world. Listen and read the article to learn more about them. Answer the questions.

Wildlife

Animal Facts

There are so many **amazing species** of animals! Each of them has their **own characteristics** and **behaviors**. They can be:

Wild Animals

These animals **live** in **forests** and **jungles** and they can be **dangerous** to human life. For example: lions, tigers, elephants, giraffes, bears **and the like**.

Domestic Animals

These animals are also called farm animals, because they are usually **found** on farms. They help with daily **labour** or by producing food and other products. For example: hens, cows, sheep, horses and the like.

Pet Animals

These animals are **kept** in the house for our **companionship** and **fun**. For example: dogs, cats, hamsters, and the like.

GLOSSARY

Amazing species: incríveis espécies.
And the like: e similares.
Behaviors: comportamentos.
Characteristics: características.
Companionship: companhia.
Dangerous: perigosos.
Found (to find): encontrados.
Forests: florestas.
Fun: diversão.
Jungles: selvas.
Kept (to keep): mantidos (manter).
Labour: trabalho.
Live (to live): vivem (viver).
Own: próprio.

a) What kind of animals are there in the article?

- ◯ Domestic animals.
- ◯ Endangered animals.
- ◯ Flying animals.
- ◯ Furry animals.
- ◯ Pets.
- ◯ Wild animals.

b) Choose the correct sentence according to the article.

- ◯ Animals have the same characteristics and behaviors.
- ◯ Each animal has its own characteristics and behaviors.

105

c) Fill in the table with the information related to each type of animal.

companionship • fun • dangerous to human life • farm animals • forests
jungles • help with labour • produce food and other products

pet animals	domestic animals	wild animals

d) Place the animals into the correct category.

hippopotamus • turtle • lion • penguin • pig • chicken
cow • dog • guinea pig • sheep • tiger • cat

pet animals	domestic animals	wild animals

2 In pairs, talk about your favorite animal.

- What is your favorite animal?
- What kind of animal is it?
- Where does it live?
- Why do you like it?

Now, choose a friend to talk about your favorite animals. Then tell the class which is your colleague's favorite animal.

His / her favorite animal is the tiger. It is a wild animal. They live in the jungle. Tigers are his / her favorite type of animal because they are beautiful and rare.

EXPLORING
- *Sing*, 2016.
- *Ferdinand*, 2017.

EXPLORING
Check out for some interesting documentaries about nature:
- https://kidworldcitizen. org/2014/11/18/incredible-nature-documentaries-kids/

CHAPTER 2

Let's practice

1) Write the correct opposite adjective.

a) fast _____

b) small _____

c) tall _____

d) nice _____

e) weak _____

f) noisy _____

> **LANGUAGE PIECE**
>
> **Opposite adjectives**
> They are adjectives that have opposite meanings:
> **tall** – short
> **big** – small
> **fast** – slow
> **fat** – thin
> **strong** – weak
> **fierce** – nice
> **new** – old
> **beautiful** – ugly

2) Complete the sentences with the correct adjectives.

a) The polar bear is a _____ animal. However, when it runs, it is _____. (heavy / light / slow / fast)

b) A domestic cat is a _____ feline animal. (fierce / nice)

c) Mice are _____ animals. (big / small)

d) The bite of a crocodile is _____. (soft / strong)

e) The giraffe is a _____ animal. A frog is _____. (tall / small / short / big)

f) The lion is the king of animals because it is _____. (fierce / nice)

g) Tigers are _____ and turtles are _____. (fast / tall / slow / short)

h) Elephants and rhinos are _____. (big / small)

3) Pair up and make sentences about animals. Look at the example, use your imagination and share them with your classmates.

> I like rabbits because they are nice and small. Tigers live in the jungle.

_____

107

4 Animals also differ in their appearance. Match the pairs of opposites.

a)
tall

slow

b)
big

short

c)
fast

nice

d)
fat

weak

e)
fierce

small

f)
strong

thin

Let's listen n' speak

1 Listen to the dialog and do as it is asked.

a) Circle the wild animals they talk about.

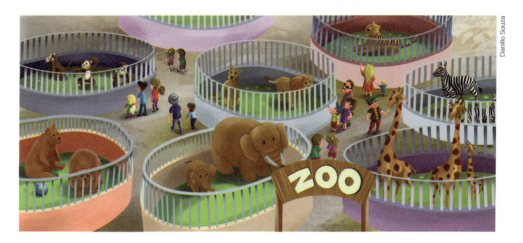

b) Which is the first animal they see?

_____

c) Who has a mane?

- ◯ Male lion.
- ◯ Female lion.
- ◯ Cub.

d) Why are the elephants hunted?

- ◯ Because of their trunk.
- ◯ Because of their size.
- ◯ Because of their tusk.

e) What is the last animal they see?

  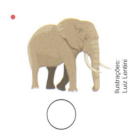

2 Have you ever been to the zoo? Talk with a partner about it.

- Do you like zoos?
- What are the good things and bad things about zoos?
- Do you think animals know they are in zoos?
- Do you feel sorry for the animals in zoos? Why or Why not?

Let's practice

1) **Complete the blanks with** that, this, those, these. **Look at the examples:**

> **That** is a lion.
> **This** is a sloth bear.
> **Those** are the elephants.
> **These** are the wheels of the bicycle.

a) What's that? Oh, _____ is my notebook.

b) What's that? _____ is his roller skate.

c) What are these? _____ are their game cards.

d) Who's this? _____ is my uncle.

e) Who's that? _____ is my cousin.

f) Who are those? _____ are our nephews.

LANGUAGE PIECE

Demonstratives
near
This   singular
These   plural
far
That   singular
Those   plural

2) **Put the words in the correct order.**

a) are / new / jeans / those / my
_____

b) that / digital camera / is / Peter's
_____

c) red scarf / is / this / a
_____

d) my / these / books / are
_____

e) jacket / is / that / my
_____

f) this / car / is / your
_____

Vocabulary hint
Demonstratives
This   That
These   Those

Let's read n' write

1) **What are endangered species?**

   a) ◯ Animals with superpopulations.   b) ◯ Animals at risk of being extinct.

2) **Do you know any kind of campaign to help endangered species? If so, which one?**

3) **Read the following campaign posters and answer the following questions.**

GLOSSARY

Aims (to aim): tem a intenção de (intentar).

Be gone: ir embora, desaparecer.

Brink of: à beira de.

Forever: para sempre.

Kind: tipo, espécie.

To halt: parar.

a) What kind of message do the posters show?

- ◯ Ask for help for a cause.
- ◯ Present some data about something.
- ◯ Give information about something.
- ◯ Explain something to people.

b) What kind of information is written on the posters?

- ◯ Endangered species numbers.
- ◯ Endangered species ask for help.
- ◯ Endangered species campaign's aim.
- ◯ Endangered species NGOs.

4 What social media element is used on the campaign posters?

_____

_____

5 What social media seems to be reproduced on the campaign posters? Why?

_____

_____

_____

6 What are the NGOs that support the campaign posters?

_____

_____

7 Read the following text about endangered species and check all the correct affirmations about it.

● ● ●   Nature   ✕

Endangered animals

Many animal species are at risk of becoming extinct, or **dying out**. Although natural causes can be a factor, humans are **largely** responsible. Activities such as **logging**, farming, and construction have destroyed many animal habitats, and illegal **hunting** has only added to the problem. [...]

GLOSSARY
Dying out: morrendo.
Hunting: caça.
Largely: amplamente.
Logging: exploração madeireira.

National Geographic Kids. Available at: <www.nationalgeographic.org/media/endangered-animals/>. Access: June 2018.

a) ◯ Natural causes are one of the factors related to species extinction, **but** not humans' actions.

b) ◯ Natural causes are one of the factors related to species extinction, **but** humans' actions are the biggest responsible.

c) ◯ Human activities such as hunting and logging helped to destroy natural environments, **so** they contributed to species extinction.

d) ◯ Human activities such as logging and farming helped to destroy natural environments, **so** they contributed to species extinction.

e) ◯ Illegal hunting **and** natural environments have contributed to species extinction.

f) ◯ Natural causes **and** illegal hunting have contributed to species extinction.

LANGUAGE PIECE
Conjunctions
- **So** Shows consequence of something.
- **But** Shows contrast between two things.
- **And** Add ideas, items, or enumerate things.

8 In your notebook, write a short paragraph talking about endangered species. Use the conjunctions and, but, and so.

9 We are going to make a campaign poster to endangered species. Brainstorm the following information:

a) What endangered species are on the campaign poster?

_____

b) What piece of information of the endangered species is on the poster?

_____

c) What NGO is going to support the campaign?

_____

d) What visual elements are on the poster?

_____

_____

e) How much text is going to be written on the poster?

_____

_____

10 Let's get to work! In a cardboard sheet make your poster with the previous information.

||| Citizenship moment |||

> **GLOSSARY**
>
> **Basin:** bacia.
> **Deaths:** mortes.
> **Lbs:** libras (unidade de medida equivalente a 453,59 gramas).
> **Lowland:** planície.
> **Major:** principal.
> **Poaching:** caça furtiva.
> **Roaming (to roam):** vagueando, ocupando (vaguear, ocupar).
> **Slipping out (to slip out):** sumindo, desaparecendo (sumir, desaparecer).
> **Threats:** ameaças.
> **Western:** ocidental.

# Let's practice

1 Complete the sentences with the text information.

a) There is _____ gorilla to every _____ human beings.

b) The major direct threat is _____.

c) The major indirect threat is _____.

d) Due to major threats, nowadays there are less than _____ gorillas left.

e) The Western Lowland Gorillas live in the _____.

f) Their average height is _____.

g) They weigh up to _____.

2 Answer according to the text.

a) What is the endangered classification of the Western Lowland Gorilla?
_____

b) What is the size of the African Congo Basin?
_____

c) How can people help?
_____

PROJECT

Research: Brazilian endangered species

Form small groups and research into endangered species that can be found in your country. Make a list that shows the name of the animal, the place where it lives, how many animals are endangered, the reasons why they are endangered and the initiatives carried out to try to revert this situation.

EXPLORING

Check out more tips on how to protect the animals and nature.

- www.thoughtco.com/save-a-species-classroom-campaign-1182037
- www.nwf.org/Home/Educational-Resources/Wildlife-Guide/
- www.thoughtco.com/things-you-can-do-to-help-wildlife-4110438

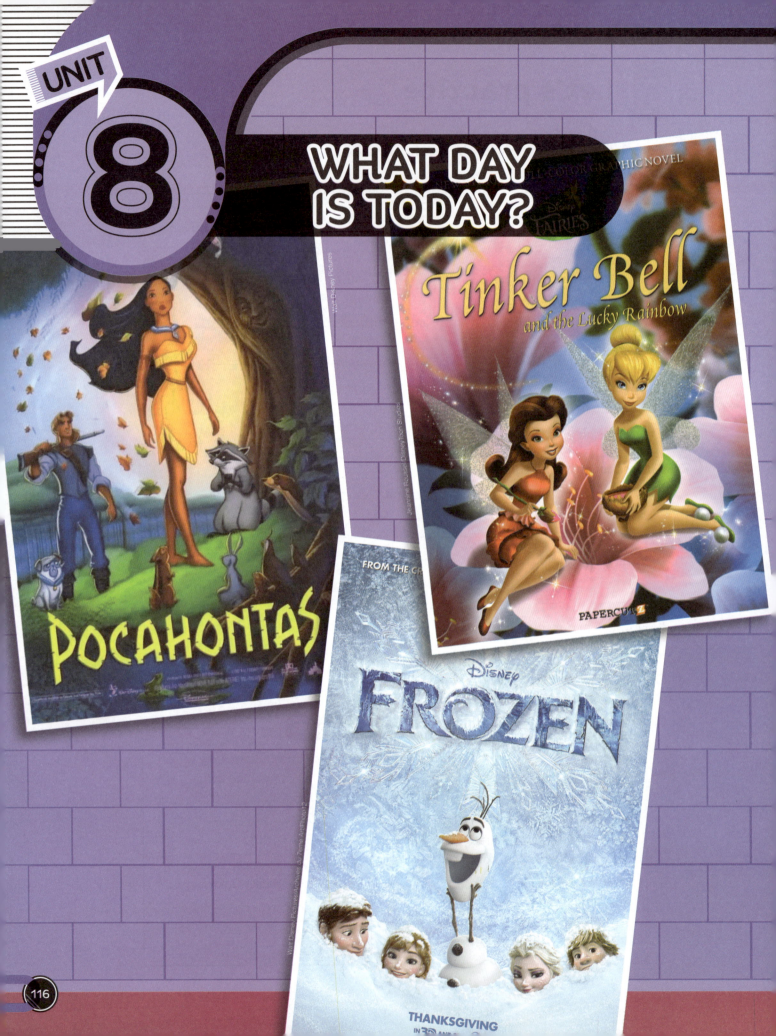

||| Get ready |||

1 Look at the posters. Number the characteristics below according to the code.

Tinker Bell – 1 • Moana – 2 • Pocahontas – 3 • Frozen – 4

a) ◯ flowers   e) ◯ sea
b) ◯ ice   f) ◯ snow
c) ◯ leaves   g) ◯ wind
d) ◯ sand   h) ◯ green landscape

2 Based on your observation of the posters, tell which season corresponds to each one:

Winter	Spring	Summer	Autumn / Fall

CHAPTER 1

Let's practice

1 Match the descriptions with the corresponding season.

a) It is when leaves fall from trees. Everything turns brown.

b) It is the season of growth. There are flowers and colors everywhere.

c) It is the coldest season. Days are shorter and greyish.

d) It is the warmest season of the year. Days are longer and brighter.

2 There are four seasons in the year. Each one lasts about three months. Can you say when they begin in Brazil? Color according to the code below.

SPRING	SUMMER	AUTUMN/FALL	WINTER
JANUARY	APRIL	JULY	OCTOBER
FEBRUARY	MAY	AUGUST	NOVEMBER
MARCH	JUNE	SEPTEMBER	DECEMBER

Let's listen n' speak

1 Listen and read the song below. Answer the following questions.

FOUR SEASONS

There are four seasons every year.
They stay three months each time.
They are very different, and it's clear!
Let's meet them in this rhyme.

At winter there is snow.
To the **South**, birds **fly**.
Plants do not **grow**,
Long are the nights.

At spring, the weather is **warmer**.
Plants and flowers **bloom**.
The **mood** is happier,
Because it is really colorful.

At summertime, the days are hot.
It's beach and vacation time!
There is sunshine in every spot,
It is sublime!

At fall, the air is **cool**.
There are leaves everywhere,
It's time to get back to school.
Autumn is in the air.

Autoral.

GLOSSARY

Bloom (to bloom): florescem (florescer).
Cool: fresco.
Fly (to fly): voam (voar).
Grow (to grow): cresce (crescer).
Mood: humor.
South: Sul.
Warmer: mais quente.

119

a) What happens with the birds in the winter?

_____

_____

b) What happens in the spring?

_____

_____

c) When is vacation time?

_____

d) When is the air cool and there are leaves everywhere?

_____

e) The sentence: *"They stay three months each time"* means:

- ( ) the year has three months.
- ( ) each season lasts three months.
- ( ) each season happens every three years.

f) The poem is related to which hemisphere? How do you know it?

_____

_____

_____

g) Find in the poem words that rhyme with:

- go _____
- lot _____
- cool _____
- each _____

2 Choose your favorite season. In trios, talk to your colleagues about it.

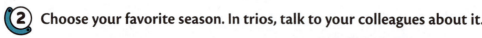

My favorite season is summer. I like it because it is warm and sunny and I can go to the beach.

120

CHAPTER 2

Let's practice

1) Number the days of the week in the correct order.

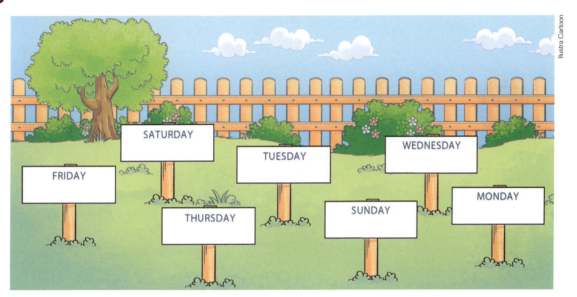

2) A day can be divided in different periods. Can you guess when we do these things? Match the activity with the correct period of the day.

a) The period when we have lunch.   • ( ) in the morning

b) The period after lunch.   • ( ) at night

c) The period when we go to bed.   • ( ) at midday

d) The period when we have dinner.   • ( ) in the afternoon

e) The period when we wake up.   • ( ) in the evening

3) Fill in with your weekly schedule.

	Monday	Tuesday	Wednesday	Thursday	Friday	Saturday	Sunday
In the morning							
At midday							
In the afternoon							
In the evening							
At night							
At midnight							

④ **Write the time and tell if it is a.m. or p.m.**

a)

_____

b)

_____

c)

_____

⑤ **What time is it? Write it down.**

a)

_____

c)

_____

b)

_____

d)

_____

LANGUAGE PIECE

Telling the time

a.m. – *ante meridian*, means before noon.

p.m. – *post meridian*, means after noon.

O'clock – entire hours.

A quarter past – fifteen minutes past an entire hour.

Half past – thirty minutes past an entire hour.

A quarter to – fifteen minutes to reach a new entire hour.

Vocabulary hint
Time expressions
O'clock   A quarter past
Half past   A quarter to

122

Let's listen n' speak

1 Listen to the dialogue and complete with the missing information.

Ben: Hey, Rachel. Do you know what time is our break?

Rachel: Hum... Our break is at _____.

Ben: Good! I'm hungry already. Do you know when the next class is?

Rachel: Let me see... it's chemistry in the laboratory at _____

_____.

Ben: Thank you! I have a day full of activities today. I have drums class

at _____.

Rachel: You'd better not arrive late to our study group today. It is at

_____.

Ben: I won't!

2 Now, listen again and answer.

  a) Where are they?

  - ◯ In the library.
  - ◯ On the beach.
  - ◯ At the cafeteria.
  - ◯ In the class.

  b) What time is the break?

  - ◯ 9:30 a.m.
  - ◯ 10:50 a.m.
  - ◯ 10:30 a.m.
  - ◯ 10:01 a.m.

  c) What is the next class? What time is it? _____

  d) Ben says: *"Good, I'm hungry already"*. The word **hungry** means...

  - ◯ ... the need to drink something.
  - ◯ ... the need to eat some food.
  - ◯ ... the need to go somewhere.

3 Pair up and make questions to a colleague about his / her daily routine.

- What time do you wake up?
- What time do you go to school?
- What time do you have breakfast / lunch / dinner?
- What time do you do your homework?
- What time do you do sports?
- What time do you go to bed?

Let's practice

1 Complete the sentences with **in**, **on** or **at**.

a) We are happy _____ Easter.
• ◯ in • ◯ on • ◯ at

b) Christmas Eve is _____ December 24th.
• ◯ in • ◯ on • ◯ at

c) Jane's birthday is _____ September.
• ◯ in • ◯ on • ◯ at

d) It happened _____ 2010.
• ◯ in • ◯ on • ◯ at

e) He came back from vacation _____ Wednesday.
• ◯ in • ◯ on • ◯ at

f) He often goes out _____ night.
• ◯ in • ◯ on • ◯ at

g) Let's meet _____ seven o'clock.
• ◯ in • ◯ on • ◯ at

h) She was born _____ June.
• ◯ in • ◯ on • ◯ at

2 Complete with the correct preposition.

a) _____ May 1st.
b) _____ the evening.
c) _____ 6:30 p.m.
d) _____ July 29th.
e) _____ April.
f) _____ midnight.

LANGUAGE PIECE

Prepositions of time
AT Precise time.
IN Months, years, long periods.
ON Days and dates.

3 Fill in the blanks with the prepositions **in**, **on** or **at**.

Janet was born _____ Rochester _____ December 22nd _____ 3 o'clock _____ the morning. Rochester is _____ New York, _____ the United States. She usually goes to classes _____ the morning _____ 8 o'clock. _____ weekends, she goes to her friend's house. She usually arrives _____ 9 o'clock _____ the evening and leaves _____ Sunday.

124

Let's read n' write

1 Answer the following questions:

a) Are you an organized person? Can you remember all of your school duties and appointments?

b) Do you know what a day planner is?

2 Take a look at Kenny's week planner and analyze it.

	Monday	Tuesday	Wednesday	Thursday
8:00 a.m. to 12:00 p.m.	SCHOOL	SCHOOL	SCHOOL	SCHOOL
1:00 p.m.				
2:00 p.m. to 3:00 p.m.	BASEBALL PRACTICE	SCHOOL GROUP WORK	BASEBALL PRACTICE	
4:00 p.m. to 5:00 p.m.			SPANISH CLASSES	SCIENCE PROJECT
6:00 p.m.				
7:00 p.m. to 8:00 p.m.	HOMEWORK	HOMEWORK	HOMEWORK	HOMEWORK
	Friday	**Saturday**	**Sunday**	**Notes**
8:00 a.m. to 12:00 p.m	SCHOOL	SCIENCE PROJECT		
1:00 p.m.			LUNCH AT GRANDMA	
2:00 p.m. to 4:00 p.m	BASEBALL PRACTICE	VISIT AUNT CLARA		
5:00 p.m. to 6:00 p.m	SPANISH CLASSES			
7:00 p.m. to 8:00 p.m	HOMEWORK			

a) When does he have baseball practice?

_____

b) When does he have Spanish classes?

_____

c) When does he have the science project?

_____

d) When does he have school group work?

_____

e) When does he have lunch at grandma's house?

_____

f) When does he have to visit his aunt?

_____

3 Go back to Kevin's week planner and tell what time he has…

a) … baseball practice.

_____

b) … homework time.

_____

c) … Spanish classes.

_____

d) … school.

_____

e) … to visit his aunt.

_____

4 What kind of information does the planner show?

a) ◯ Full date.   **d)** ◯ Activity.

b) ◯ Week day.   **e)** ◯ Place.

c) ◯ Time.   **f)** ◯ People.

5 What about practicing how to be more organized? Follow the instructions to create your own school planner.

How to organize your day planner for school

Steps

1. Name your **planner**.
2. Write out **sections** for every subject / course you take.
3. Make your planner a part of your **daily routine**.
4. Fill in your **assignments' due dates** as soon as you get them.
5. Learn to use the **backward planning**.
6. Use the color **coding system**. It will keep your planner and you more organized.
7. Put everything in your planner. That includes homework, tests, parties, shopping, conferences, etc.
8. Use colorful **sticky-note flags** to mark your events.
9. Don't **discard** old pages. You never know if it will **come in handy**.

GLOSSARY

Assignments' due dates: datas de entrega de trabalhos.

Backward planning: planejamento regressivo.

Coding system: sistema de código.

Come in handy: ser útil.

Daily routine: rotina diária.

Discard: jogar fora.

Planner: cronograma, lista de afazeres.

Sections: seções.

Sticky-note flags: notas de papel; etiquetas de colar.

Based on: <www.wikihow.com/Organize-Your-Day-Planner-for-School>. Access: June 2018.

WEEKLY SCHEDULE

	MONDAY	TUESDAY	WEDNESDAY	THURSDAY	FRIDAY	SATURDAY	SUNDAY
8:00 am							
9:00 am							
10:00 am							
11:00 am							
12:00 pm							
1:00 pm							
2:00 pm							
3:00 pm							
4:00 pm							
5:00 pm							
6:00 pm							
7:00 pm							
8:00 pm							

CHAPTER 4

||| Tying in |||

Time zone

The adoption of the international time zone in 1912, allowed the determination of the time in every region.

WHAT IT IS AND WHAT IT REPRESENTS

The Earth surface is divided in 24 time zones each of 15° of longitude.

The time zone are centered on the meridian at longitude 0°, 15°, 45°, etc., East and West respectively.

Inside a time zone, all places have the same time.

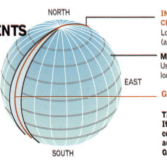

INTERNATIONAL LINE CHANGE OF THE DATE
Located at 180° from Greenwich (aprox.)

MERIDIAN
Used to determine the longitude of a place.

GREENWICH MERIDIAN

TIME ZONE 0
It was adopted as a time zone 0, centred in the first meridian going across the Royal Observatory of Greenwich, United Kingdom.

TIME EQUIVALENCES
When in the time zone 0 is 12:00, according to the international time zones, the time in the following city in the world is:

CITY	TIME ZONE	TIME
WASHINGTON USA	5 HS WEST	7:00
BUENOS AIRES Argentina	3 HS WEST	9:00
PRAIA Green Cape	1 HS WEST	11:00
ROME Italy	1 HS EAST	13:00
BEIJING China	8 HS EAST	20:00
SYDNEY Australia	10 HS EAST	22:00

TIME ZONES IN THE WORLD

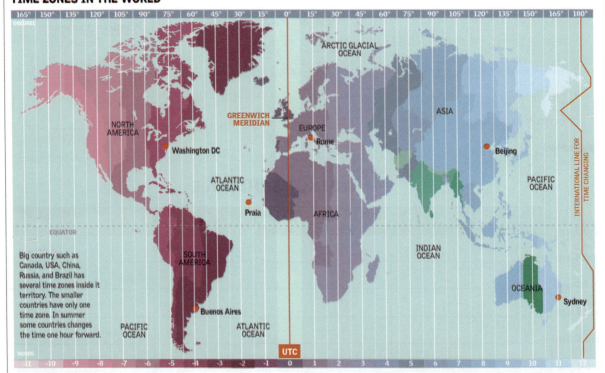

Big country such as Canada, USA, China, Russia, and Brazil has several time zones inside it territory. The smaller countries have only one time zone. In summer some countries changes the time one hour forward.

› THE TIME BALL

Constructed in 1833, the Greenwich ball was one of the first visual signals. It was used to synchronize the chronometer of the ship crews.

1 The wicker ball, 60 cm of diameter, used to be lifted up five minutes before signaling time.

2 At the proper time it used to be left down.

› ATOMIC WATCHES

In 1967 the **atomic second** was adopted as a legal physical time, based on the caesium atom 133. In 1933 a universal coordinated time was adopted (UTC) as a time scale used in normal life having the atomic second as unit. This originates from the date of 230 atomic watches of 65 labs distributed around the world by the International office of Weight and Measures. The NIST F-1, an atomic caesium watch located in Colorado (USA), is considered to most precise in the word. It can work for 20 million years without ever getting too late to or to early of a single second.

||| GLOSSARY

Crews: tripulações.

Lifted down (to be lifted down): baixada (ser baixada).

Lifted up (to be lifted up): levantada (ser levantada).

Wicker ball: bola de vime.

Let's practice

1. Read the text and answer the questions.

a) How is the Earth surface divided?

_____

_____

b) What is the meridian used for?

_____

_____

c) What does the international time zone permit?

_____

_____

d) What time is it in London?

_____

_____

e) What time is it in San Francisco?

_____

_____

_____

EXPLORING

Time Zones, by Edward Miller III. Holiday House.

- *At the Same Moment, around the World*, by Clotilde Perrin. Chronicle Books; Rei/Ma edition.

PROJECT

Brazilian Time Zones

Team up, research about the different time zones in Brazil, and exchange the information with your classmates.

EXPLORING

Time Zones

- http://easyscienceforkids.com/all-about-the-time-zone/

REVIEW

1) Rewrite the names of the animals from the box below in the correct place.

> ferret • dog • cat • bird • hippopotamus • monkey • zebra • pig
> lion • giraffe • cow • chicken • turtle • penguin • guinea pig • sheep

farm animals	wild animals	pets

2) Rewrite the time using **a.m.** or **p.m.**:

a) nine in the morning _____

b) eleven at night _____

c) midday _____

d) one in the afternoon _____

e) midnight _____

f) six in the evening _____

3) Look at the month sequences and circle the odd one out.

a) March   April   May   June   December   August   September

b) January   November   March   April   May   June   July

c) June   July   August   September   February   November   December

d) April   May   June   July   August   September   March

4) Write the opposites.

a) tall _____

b) big _____

c) fast _____

d) fat _____

e) strong _____

f) fierce _____

130

5) Draw the clock hands according to the time mentioned.

a) It's five o'clock.

c) It's a quarter to eleven.

b) It's a quarter past one.

d) It's three thirty.

6) Put the words in the correct order.

a) are / those / his / umbrellas / new

_____

b) pets / these / their / are

_____

c) is / that / Sandy's / backpack / new

_____

d) house / this / my / is

_____

e) are / those / parents / Jason's and Bruce's

_____

f) my / these / favorite / are / song writers

_____

DO NOT FORGET!

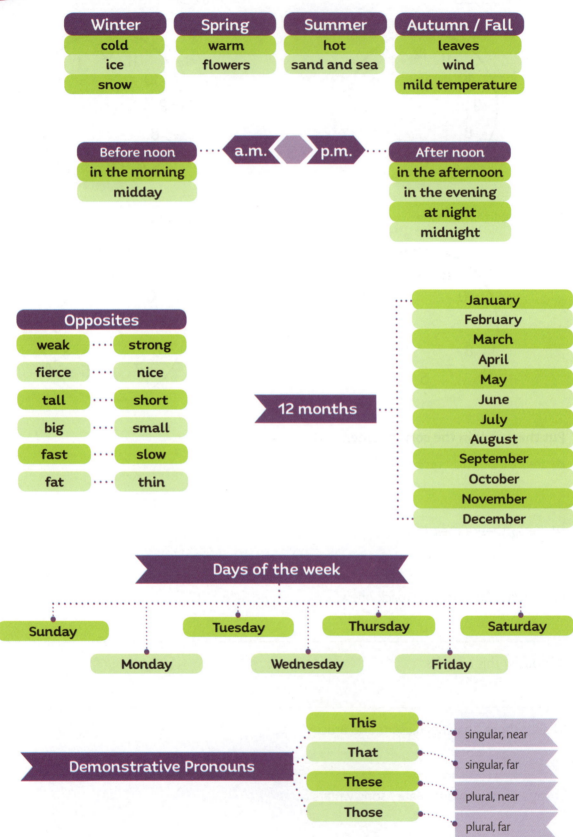

OVERCOMING CHALLENGES

(ENEM – 2010)

Questão 94

Definidas pelos países-membros da Organização das Nações Unidas e por organizações internacionais, as metas de desenvolvimento do milênio envolvem oito objetivos a serem alcançados até 2015. Apesar da diversidade cultural, esses objetivos, mostrados na imagem, são comuns ao mundo todo, sendo dois deles:

Programa das Nações Unidas para o Desenvolvimento

a) O combate à AIDS e a melhoria do ensino universitário.

b) A redução da mortalidade adulta e a criação de parcerias globais.

c) A promoção da igualdade de gêneros e a erradicação da pobreza.

d) A parceria global para o desenvolvimento e a valorização das crianças.

e) A garantia da sustentabilidade ambiental e o combate ao trabalho infantil.

WORKBOOK

Unit 1

1) Write the short form.

a) She is _____

b) They are _____

c) It is _____

d) That is _____

e) I am not _____

2) Complete with am, is or are.

a) Miley Cyrus _____ a famous singer.

b) My friends and I _____ always happy.

c) I _____ a good student.

d) My family _____ big.

3) Practice with a classmate. Use your creativity and practice forming sentences about friends and family using the verb to be.

_____
_____
_____
_____

4) Make questions using am, is or are.

a) _____ you and Bill friends?

b) _____ this your pet dog?

c) _____ they your cousins?

d) _____ I late for school?

5) Write the numbers in figures and then write them in full. Look at the example.

Your age: **10 – ten**.

a) Your birthday (day): _____.

b) Your birthday (month): _____.

c) Your age: _____.

d) This month: _____.

6) **Complete the form with your personal information and then complete the other form with a friend's personal information.**

my information		my classmate information	
First name		First name	
Last name		Last name	
Middle name		Middle name	
Nickname		Nickname	

7) **Let's practice the greetings. Choose the best option.**

a)

Nice _____ you.

- ◯ morning
- ◯ to morning
- ◯ meet
- ◯ to meet

c)

You get to school at 7 a.m. and meet your teacher.

- ◯ Good morning!
- ◯ Good evening!
- ◯ Good afternoon!
- ◯ Good night!

b)

How are you? – I'm _____.

- ◯ fine, thank you
- ◯ good bye
- ◯ good afternoon
- ◯ nice to meet you

d)

You get home at 7 p.m. and meet your brother.

- ◯ Good morning!
- ◯ Good evening!
- ◯ Good afternoon!
- ◯ Good night!

135

WORKBOOK

||| Unit 2 |||

1) Write the missing words in the correct place.

This is my _____. This is John, my _____, and this is Tracy, my _____. I have an older _____ and no _____. I am the only girl. We have a nice _____ and a sleepy _____. We live near our _____. We are a very happy family.

| family |
| dog |
| mother |
| sister |
| cat |
| grandparents |
| father |
| brother |

2) Circle the correct possessive adjective. Look at the example.

> I'm Vania and this is **MY** bicycle.
> **She** is Vania and this is **HER** bicycle.

a) My mother is Maria and this is (his / her) bag.

b) They are Ramona and Arthur and this is (its / their) house.

c) I am Marcela and this is (my / her) bedroom.

d) We are Bernardo and Samira and this is (their / our) favorite animation movie.

e) This is my cousin and (my / his) name is Paul.

f) Abe is a cat and (his / its) favorite food is fish.

3) Write the correct possessive adjectives.

a) Our names are Karen and Robert. This is _____ father.

b) James and Vanessa live with _____ parents.

c) Tobby likes _____ video game very much.

d) My name is Annie. This is _____ aunt, Louisa.

e) _____ name is Alex.

136

4 Write sentences using the given information. Look at the example.

> Susana / girl / book   She is Susana and this is her book.

a) Tom / boy / skateboard

_____

b) Greg and Sam / brothers / family

_____

c) Leslie / girl / notebook

_____

d) Jay and I / students / school

_____

5 Match the question word with its meaning.

a) Who   • things

b) What   • person / people

c) Where   • time

d) When   • place

6 Now, write a question using each question word from the previous exercise.

_____

_____

_____

_____

7 Circle the correct option.

a) (Who / When) do you go to school?

b) (What / Who) is your teacher?

c) (What / Who) is your favorite color?

d) (What / Where) are the kids?

137

WORKBOOK

||| Unit 3 |||

1 Look at Darla's daily activities and answer the following questions about it.

a) At what time does she brush her teeth? _____

b) At what time does she read? _____

c) At what time does she have dinner? _____

d) At what time does she go to bed? _____

2 Look at Darla's daily activities again and change the following sentences into their negative and interrogative forms.

a) Darla wakes up at 7:00.

Negative: _____

Interrogative: _____

b) Darla has breakfast at 7:30.

Negative: _____

Interrogative: _____

c) Darla goes to school at 2:00 p.m.

Negative: _____

Interrogative: _____

d) Darla has dinner at 6:00 p.m.

Negative: _____

Interrogative: _____

e) Darla goes to bed at 9:00 p.m.

Negative: _____

Interrogative: _____

3 Complete the following sentences with the correct preposition and one adverb of frequency. Do not repeat the adverbs of frequency.

at • in • on

always • usually • often • never • rarely • frequently • sometimes • hardly ever

a) I _____ wake up early _____ Saturdays.

b) My friends _____ go to work _____ December.

c) Ashley _____ feeds her pet _____ midnight.

d) The Smiths _____ get up _____ 7:00.

e) My brother and I _____ play outside _____ the winter.

f) Bob _____ visits his grandparents _____ July 4th.

4 Complete the sentences below with the correct present simple form of the verbs.

a) We _____ our pet in the morning and at night. (to feed)

b) Helena _____ dinner with her family every day. (to have)

c) I never _____ to work by car. (to go)

d) He always _____ soccer on Saturdays. (to play)

e) Patrick usually _____ TV at night. (to watch)

f) Clara hardly ever _____ a shower before school. (to take)

WORKBOOK

||| Unit 4 |||

1) Complete the dialogues with the correct wh-word.

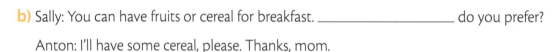

where
what
which

a) Mary: Hi! _____ is your name?

John: My name is John. Nice to meet you!

b) Sally: You can have fruits or cereal for breakfast. _____ do you prefer?

Anton: I'll have some cereal, please. Thanks, mom.

c) Jason: Hi, Cindy. Tell me, _____ do you study?

Cindy: I study at Santa Monica College. It's near that big supermarket.

2) Look at the following flags. Can you say which country they belong to? Complete the sentences with the correct country and nationality.

a)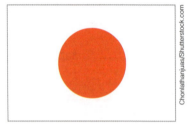

Mitsuko is from _____.

She is _____.

c)

Carlos is from _____.

He is _____.

b)

Joseph is from _____.

He is _____.

d)

Ann is from _____.

She is _____.

3) Look at exercise 2 and write each country language.

a) _____

b) _____

c) _____

d) _____

140

4. Complete the crossword puzzle below with the correct nationalities.

Down

1. I love food from Mexico. Actually, _____ food is my favorite!

2. That blouse is from India. I have many _____ clothes.

3. That singer is from Russia! _____ singers are not very famous.

Across

4. My new teacher is from France. She is _____.

5. My grandpa is _____. My grandma is from Italy too.

6. Which is your favorite _____ city, New York or Miami?

7. People from China are _____.

5. Complete with the correct form of the possessive case.

a) My teachers _____ cars are on the street.

b) Michael _____ house is just around the corner.

c) Our mother _____ room is very big.

d) The students _____ books are on that desk.

6. Write the numbers in full, ordinal or cardinal forms according to what is missing.

	cardinal	ordinal
1	one	
12		twelfth
17	seventeen	

WORKBOOK

||| Unit 5 |||

1 Complete the sentences with the correct present continuous form.

a) I _____ chess. (negative – to play)

b) _____ they _____ yoga? (interrogative – to do)

c) Mia _____ fishing. (affirmative – to go)

d) _____ Ivete _____ chess? (interrogative – to play)

e) Ray and Hugo _____ archery. (negative – to do)

f) We _____ karate. (affirmative – to do)

2 Form sentences in the negative form using the present continuous.

a) You / not / handball / playing

_____

b) He / skating / not / is / roller

_____

c) not / She / reading / is / the newspaper

_____

d) a documentary / We / not / are / watching

_____

e) cards / are / They / playing / not

_____

3 Rewrite the sentences according to the indications: **A** (affirmative), **N** (negative) or **I** (interrogative).

a) The kids are climbing a wall. (**N**)

_____

b) Noriko isn't reading. (**A**)

_____

c) They are cooking. (**I**)

_____

d) Geraldo is swimming. (**N**)

_____

4 Match the questions with the right answers.

a) Is Sheila doing ballet?

b) Is Sonia playing board games?

c) Are the kids roller skating?

d) Are you going bowling?

e) Is your dad watching a movie?

f) Are you doing gymnastics?

- ( ) No, I am not.
- ( ) No, she is not. She is doing yoga.
- ( ) Yes, she is. She loves playing chess.
- ( ) No, he is not.
- ( ) No, they are not.
- ( ) Yes, I am. Bowling is a great hobby!

5 Distribute the activities into the correct group.

dancing	bowling	basketball	tennis
archery	gymnastics	tai chi	fishing
ballet	board games	cards	karate
skating	yoga	surfing	football
chess	taekwondo	soccer	

do	go	play

6 Choose two options of each column and write sentences about what you are doing these days.

_____

_____

WORKBOOK

||| Unit 6 |||

1) Unscramble the letters to discover the parts of a house.

a) gvliin ormo _____

b) ginnid moor _____

c) moordbe _____

d) tcenhik _____

e) darykcab _____

f) erdnag _____

2) Write two items you can find in each of the previous places.

a) Living room: _____

b) Dining room: _____

c) Bedroom: _____

d) Kitchen: _____

e) Backyard: _____

f) Garden: _____

3) Circle the correct options.

a) There is a microwave in the _____. (bathroom / kitchen)

b) _____ birds in the garden. (There is / There are)

c) _____ some juice in the refrigerator. (There is / There are)

d) _____ two beds in the bedroom. (There is / There are)

e) _____ a couch in the living room. (There is / There are)

f) There aren't any sinks in the _____. (dining room / bathroom)

144

4) Rewrite only the wrong sentences.

a) There is a car in the dining room.

_____

b) There is a rug in the garden.

_____

c) There are some chairs in the living room.

_____

d) There is a stove in the attic.

_____

e) There is a toilet in the bathroom.

_____

f) There are two sinks in the kitchen.

_____

5) Match the columns.

a) at

- ◯ the wall
- ◯ my bed

b) in

- ◯ Canada
- ◯ the door

c) on

- ◯ the beach
- ◯ the bus stop

6) Put the words in order to form sentences.

a) books / on / there are / the bookshelf / some

_____

b) on / there are / my bed / some / magazines

_____

c) there is / the garage / a / trashcan / in

_____

d) armchair / the living room / an / there is / in

_____

7) Rewrite the sentences in A (affirmative) or N (negative) forms and complete with there is / there are and some / any.

a) _____ paintings on the wall. (A)

b) _____ water on the table. (N)

c) _____ jackets in my wardrobe. (A)

d) _____ people at the bus stop. (N)

WORKBOOK

||| Unit 7 |||

1. Find 8 animals in the wordsearch and complete the list.

H	S	Y	M	I	V	X	N	M	W	Y	N	Z
Y	X	T	C	I	Z	E	B	R	A	W	D	N
E	S	I	I	Q	M	R	A	A	J	C	T	I
P	A	G	B	R	T	P	Q	B	W	T	U	F
S	I	E	Q	J	S	I	Y	B	T	F	I	T
U	G	R	R	S	R	X	P	I	G	N	Z	U
H	I	P	O	H	C	A	J	T	B	E	P	G
H	o	R	D	E	B	F	W	E	H	N	B	N
F	E	R	R	E	T	R	B	D	E	F	Q	C
N	V	I	P	P	E	P	Z	H	E	T	A	K
G	W	I	L	T	Y	P	F	O	U	R	T	H
P	T	P	E	N	G	U	I	N	R	Y	T	B
R	G	P	H	Q	N	W	Q	K	P	G	T	L
B	N	X	I	M	O	N	K	E	Y	R	J	X
Y	U	T	P	E	V	T	J	S	M	E	C	A

a) _____
b) _____
c) _____
d) _____
e) _____
f) _____
g) _____
h) _____

2. Choose the best option.

a) They live in the jungle:
- ◯ chickens.
- ◯ tigers.
- ◯ sheep.

b) They are dangerous:
- ◯ guinea pigs.
- ◯ turtles.
- ◯ lions.

c) It produces a lot of milk:
- ◯ hippopotamus.
- ◯ cat.
- ◯ cow.

d) Pet animal:
- ◯ dog.
- ◯ hippopotamus.
- ◯ tiger.

e) Lives on farms:
- ◯ chicken.
- ◯ monkey.
- ◯ zebra.

f) Lives in the savana:
- ◯ horse.
- ◯ giraffe.
- ◯ guinea pig.

3 Rewrite the sentences and substitute the underlined word for a word with the opposite meaning.

a) Look at that big animal over there!

___

b) My Russian friend is that strong man by the door.

___

c) What a cute fat pig!

___

d) Look at that tiger: it looks fierce!

___

4 Complete the gaps with so, but or and.

a) My father will go to the supermarket to buy some fruits _____ some milk.

b) Christine is my friend, _____ I don't like her very much.

c) I studied a lot, _____ I think I will get a good grade on my test.

d) Anita needs to buy a new notebook _____ a backpack.

e) I study in the same class as John, _____ we are not friends.

f) The school year is over, _____ I think it is time to enjoy summer vacations.

5 Using the information in parenthesis, complete the gaps with the words from the box.

> this • that • these • those

a) _____ is my teacher, Caroline. (Singular, near)

b) _____ are my classmates, Albert and Andrea. (Plural, far)

c) _____ book on the table over there is really fun. (Singular, far)

d) _____ are my parents! We are a happy family! (Plural, near)

WORKBOOK

||| Unit 8 |||

1 What is the season?

a)

It's _____.

b)

It's _____.

c)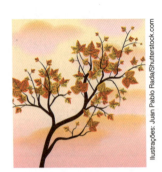

It's _____.

d)

It's _____.

2 Check the two options that best relate to each season.

a) spring
- ◯ really cold temperature
- ◯ flowers
- ◯ warm temperature
- ◯ snow

b) autumn / fall
- ◯ really cold temperature
- ◯ leaves
- ◯ wind
- ◯ ice

c) summer
- ◯ really cold temperature
- ◯ leaves
- ◯ hot temperature
- ◯ sand and sea

d) winter
- ◯ really cold temperature
- ◯ leaves
- ◯ mild temperature
- ◯ ice and snow

3 Unscramble the words and write the names of the months.

a) mrcah _____

b) jnue _____

c) setmbeper _____

d) deeebcmr _____

e) jaaurny _____

f) mya _____

g) auusgt _____

h) ooctebr _____

i) aripl _____

j) jluy _____

k) freubray _____

l) neobvmer _____

4 What time is it?

a)

_____

c)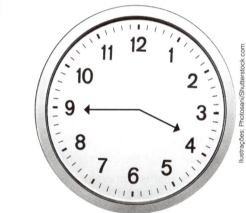

_____

b)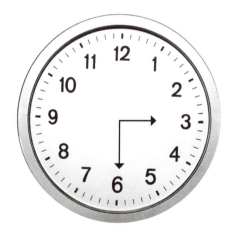

_____

d)

_____

149

EXPERT'S POINT I

Psychology

The "Do You Know?" 20 Questions About Family Stories

Here is one way to start telling and sharing family stories.

I have been blogging about the value of family stories, and research from *The Family Narratives Lab* showing that children and adolescents who know more of their family stories show **higher well-being** on multiple measures, including higher self-esteem, higher academic competence, higher social competence, and **fewer behavior** problems. So how can you start sharing your family stories?

Marshall Duke and I developed the *"Do You Know …?"* **scale**, sometimes called *"The 20 Questions"* that **tap into** different kinds of family stories. These questions are designed as a starting point for **sharing** family stories. Please keep in mind that it is not knowledge of these specific facts that is important – it is the process of families sharing stories about their lives that is important. So these questions are a way **to begin** to ask and to tell, and to begin a family tradition of sharing the stories of our lives.

GLOSSARY

Act: agir.
Awards: prêmios.
Background: origem.
Behavior: comportamento.
Fewer: poucos.
Grew up (to grow up): cresceu (crescer).
Grumpy: rabugento.
Higher: mais alto.
Illnesses: doenças.
Injuries: machucados.
Look like: ser parecido com.
Met (to meet): encontrou (encontrar).
Received (to receive): recebido (receber).
Scale: escala.
Sharing (to share): compartilhar.
Source: fonte.
Tap into: tocar.
To begin: começar.
Well-being: bem-estar.
Went on (to go on): aconteceu (acontecer).
Were being born (to be born): nasceu (nascer).
Were married (to be married): casou (casar).
Whose: de quem.

1. Do you know how your parents **met**?
2. Do you know where your mother **grew up**?
3. Do you know where your father grew up?
4. Do you know where some of your grandparents grew up?
5. Do you know where some of your grandparents met?

6. Do you know where your parents **were married**?
7. Do you know what **went on** when you **were being born**?
8. Do you know the **source** of your name?
9. Do you know some things about what happened when your brothers or sisters were being born?
10. Do you know which person in your family you **look** most **like**?
11. Do you know which person in the family you **act** most like?
12. Do you know some of the **illnesses** and **injuries** that your parents experienced when they were younger?
13. Do you know some of the lessons that your parents learned from good or bad experiences?
14. Do you know some things that happened to your mom or dad when they were in school?
15. Do you know the national **background** of your family (such as English, German, Russian, etc.)?
16. Do you know some of the jobs that your parents had when they were young?
17. Do you know some **awards** that your parents **received** when they were young?
18. Do you know the names of the schools that your mom went to?
19. Do you know the names of the schools that your dad went to?
20. Do you know about a relative **whose** face "froze" in a **grumpy** position because he or she did not smile enough?

I hope these questions help you to begin to learn more of your family stories and share them across the generations.

Expert's profile

Robyn Fivush, Ph.D.

Professor of Psychology at Emory University, in Atlanta, United States. Her research is focused on family storytelling and the relations among memory, narrative, identity, trauma, and coping.

PROJECT

"Do you know?" interview

Choose four questions from the "*Do you know?*" list and in small groups take turns asking to one another and listening to the answers. Each student will share with the class one thing they talked about.

Robyn Fivush. The "Do You Know?" 20 questions about family stories. *Psychology Today*. Available at: <www.psychologytoday.com/blog/the-stories-our-lives/201611/the-do-you-know-20-questions-about-family-stories>. Access: June 2018.

EXPERT'S POINT II

Wild life

Scientists Say: Zooplankton

These are tiny, floating predators of the sea

BETHANY BROOKSHIRE / FEB 26, 2018 — 6:30 AM EST

These brilliant beings are all different types of zooplankton, tiny animals that float in the sea.

Zooplankton (noun, "Zoh-uh-PLANK-ton")

These are a type of plankton – tiny organisms that <u>drift</u> freely in the sea. These <u>critters</u> can be so <u>tiny</u> you need a microscope to see them up to about the size of a <u>flea</u>. Some zooplankton remain that tiny forever. Others are the baby version of species that <u>grow up</u> to <u>become</u> larger animals, such as fish or crabs.

Some plankton – called phytoplankton – are plant-like. They produce energy from the sun. But zooplankton are <u>predators</u>. They <u>prey</u> on phytoplankton and on other, smaller zooplankton. But these tiny, <u>fearsome hunters</u> are <u>hunted</u> themselves. Zooplankton are part of a balanced diet for many fish, birds and whales.

GLOSSARY

Become: tornar-se.
Chilled: refrigerado, gelado.
Critters: animais, bichos.
Dine: jantar.
Drift: flutuar.
Fearsome: temíveis.
Flea: pulga.
Grow up: crescer.
Hunted (to hunt): caçado (caçar).
Hunters: caçadores.
Predators: predadores.
Prey: presa.
Tiny: minúsculo.

In a sentence

In the Arctic, some zooplankton prefer their food <u>chilled</u> and <u>dine</u> on sea-ice algae. […]

Bethany Brookshire. Scientists say: zooplankton. *Science News for Students*. Available at: <www.sciencenewsforstudents.org/blog/scientists-say/scientists-say-zooplankton>. Access: Apr. 2018.

Expert's profile

PROJECT

What is a plankton?

Team up and research about planktons, especially the types found in the Brazilian ecosystem. Then, exchange the information with the other groups and decide on the most interesting findings about it.

After all the information exchanged, make a model of these planktons.

Bethany Brookshire

Has a B.S. in biology and a B.A. in philosophy from The College of William and Mary, and a Ph.D. in physiology and pharmacology from Wake Forest University School of Medicine. She is the guest editor of *The Open Laboratory Anthology of Science Blogging*, 2009, and the winner of the Society for Neuroscience Next Generation Award and the Three Quarks Daily Science Writing Award, among others. She blogs at **Eureka! Lab** and at **Scicurious**.

FOCUS ON CULTURE I

HOUSING, HEALTH AND SCHOLAR PERFORMANCE

263 MILLION CHILDREN, ADOLESCENTS AND YOUTH ARE OUT OF SCHOOL

According to the United Nations Educational, Scientific and Cultural Organization (Unesco), in 2016, 263 million children, adolescents and youth were out of school – this is almost one-fifth of the global population of this age group.

WHY?

THE HIGH OUT-OF-SCHOOL RATES FOR OLDER STUDENTS CAN BE EXPLAINED BY POVERTY AND A VARIETY OF OTHER REASONS:

Many youth never had a chance to attend school when they were younger.

Upper secondary education is often not compulsory.

NOT COMPULSORY

Upper secondary school-age youth may choose employment over continuing their education.

BRAZIL

8 IS THE COUNTRY'S AVERAGE NUMBER OF YEARS OF STUDY
11.8 MILLION OF ILLITERATE PEOPLE AMONG THE POPULATION THAT IS 15 YEARS OLD OR MORE

Only **51%** of the population completed studies in primary school.

Only **26.3%** of the population completed secondary school.

Only **15.3%** of the population finished college.

PROBLEMS

WHY DO CHILDREN AND YOUNG PEOPLE SKIP SCHOOL?

Family worried about basic survival needs, such as food.

Poor health and medical care.

Lack of clothing and supplies.

Lack of transportation.

PROJECT

Pie Chart and Donation Campaign

Research the following topics and construct a pie chart with the results of your investigation.
- In your city, how many kids and teens are out of school?
- How many kids and teens live in your city?
- Why are these kids and teens out of school? What are the main reasons?
- What can be done to help these people go back to school?
- How can we prevent other kids and teens from abandoning school?

Then, work in groups and prepare a school material donation campaign. This campaign should involve all students in your own school. Collect all school material donations and help one of these institutions you have researched about.

FOCUS ON CULTURE II

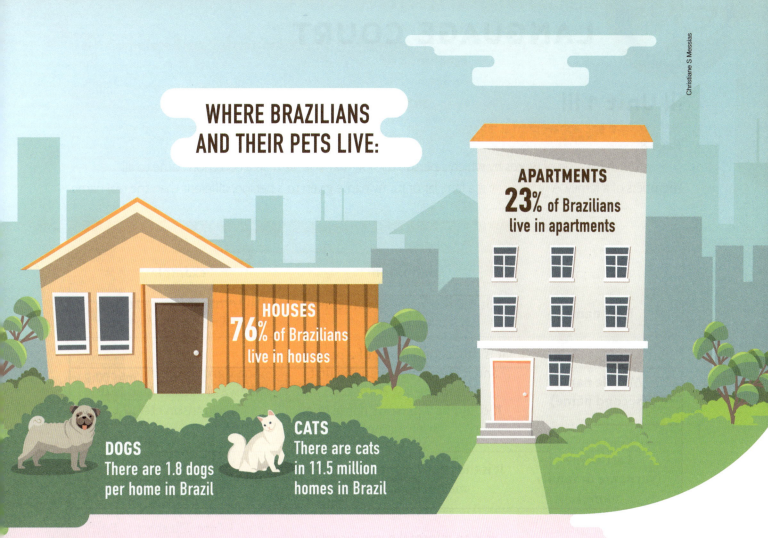

WHERE BRAZILIANS AND THEIR PETS LIVE:

HOUSES 76% of Brazilians live in houses

APARTMENTS 23% of Brazilians live in apartments

DOGS There are 1.8 dogs per home in Brazil

CATS There are cats in 11.5 million homes in Brazil

🐾 PETS AROUND THE WORD (MILLIONS)
🐾 PETS IN BRAZIL (MILLIONS)

	DOGS	BIRDS	CATS	FISHES
World	360.8	205.2	271.9	655.8
Brazil	52.2	37.9	22.1	18

PROJECT

Homeless pets
Discuss the following topics with your classmates:
- Why are there so many homeless animals?
- How can we help homeless animals?
- Are there any NGOs or government institutions near your school that work helping homeless animals?
- What are their names? How do they help animals?
- Can you and your classmates help any of these institutions and organizations? If so, how?

Then, working in groups, make a poster teaching people how to help homeless animals. Don't forget to mention information about institutions that can really help and be helped!

Based on: IBGE – População de animais de estimação no Brasil – 2013 – Em milhões, available at: <http://www.agricultura.gov.br/assuntos/camaras-setoriais-tematicas/documentos/camaras-tematicas/insumos-agropecuarios/anos-anteriores/ibge-populacao-de-animais-de-estimacao-no-brasil-2013-abinpet-79.pdf>; Brasileiros têm 52 milhões de cães e 22 milhões de gatos, aponta IBGE, available at: <http://g1.globo.com/natureza/noticia/2015/06/brasileiros-tem-52-milhoes-de-caes-e-22-milhoes-de-gatos-aponta-ibge.html>. Acces: May 2018.

LANGUAGE COURT

||| Unit 1 |||

Page 8

A **name** is a set of words by which a person is known. A **last name** is a common name to all members of a family. A **nickname** is a familiar or funny name given to a person, different than the real name.

	Parts of a name	
	definition	**example**
First name	It is the first name of someone's full name.	Paul, Robert, Amanda, Yuki, Caroline, Peter, Mark etc.
Middle name (second name)	It is the second name of a person and it comes between the first and the last names. It could be a person's name or a family name.	Ana **Carolina** Duarte; Peter **Edward** Pecker; Alan **Hill** Johnson etc.
Last name (surname or family name)	It is the family name used by the members of a family.	Pecker, Stannis, Schrinder, Viamonte, Sanches, Takaki, Bolt, Silva etc.
Nickname	It is an informal name, usually given by family or friends.	Peter – **Pete**; Elizabeth – **Beth**; Ronaldo – "**Fenômeno**", **Ronaldinho** etc.

Pages 11 to 13

Verb to be				
affirmative Form		negative Form		interrogative form
full form	short form	full form	short form	full form
I am	I'm	I am not	I'm not	Am I…?
He is She is It is	He's She's It's	He is not She is not It is not	He isn't She isn't It isn't	Is he…? Is she…? Is it…?
You are We are They are	You're We're They're	You are not We are not They are not	You aren't We aren't They aren't	Are you…? Are we…? Are they…?

examples		
I **am** at school. Daniel **is** in a balloon. Emma and Greg **are** friends.	I **am not ('m not)** at home. She **is not (isn't)** on a bus. They **are not (aren't)** brother and sister.	**Am I** at home? **Is he** in a balloon? **Are they** friends?

Pay attention!

We	You
Plural. Means a group that the speaker belongs to.	Singular or plural. Means a person (or more than one) to whom we speak.
Peter, Carol, Yuki, Bob and I are friends. **We** are friends.	Are Edward and Bob friends? Are you friends? Are you a dentist?

Remember:

Names can be substituted by the **personal pronouns**.

HE: Peter **Peter** is a rugby player. **He** is a rugby player.	**SHE:** Lily **Lily** saw a bird in the sky. **She** saw a bird in the sky.	**IT:** A dog, an airplane, etc. **A dog** was in the garage. **It** was in the garage.	**THEY:** Paul and Bob / the students / the birds, etc. **The students** eat lunch every day. **They** eat lunch every day.

Page 14

Numbers			
Base numbers	0 1 2 3 4	zero one two three four	5 6 7 8 9	five six seven eight nine
"Teen" numbers	10 11 12 13	ten eleven twelve thirteen	14 15 16 17 18 19	fourteen fifteen sixteen seventeen eighteen nineteen
The following number	20		twenty	

||| Unit 2 |||

Page 22

A *family* is formed by a group of people related to one another and might have a common ancestor, who love, trust, care and look out for each other.

Family members	
mother + father	parents
grandmother + grandfather	grandparents
son + daughter son + son daughter + daughter	children
boy + boy	brothers or siblings
girl + girl	sisters or siblings
boy + girl	brother and sister or siblings

Pages 25 and 26

Question words		
	function	example
What	asks for information about something	What is your name?
Who	asks about people (subject)	Who is your father?
Where	asks about a place or position	Where are they?
When	asks about time or dates	When is your birthday?
Why	asks the reason of something	Why are you going out?

Page 27

Possessive adjectives	
Shows ownership. The possessive adjective needs to agree with the possessor and not with the thing that is possessed. Like all adjectives in English, they are always located in front of the noun they refer to. Possessive adjectives say WHAT belongs to WHOM.	This is my ball.

Possessive adjectives	
I	My
You	Your
He	His
She	Her
It	Its
We	Our
You	Your
They	Their

||| Unit 3 |||

Page 41

Adverbs of frequency are used to describe the frequency an activity is done or something happens. The most common of them are **always**, **usually**, **frequently**, **often**, **sometimes**, **rarely**, **hardly ever**, and **never**.

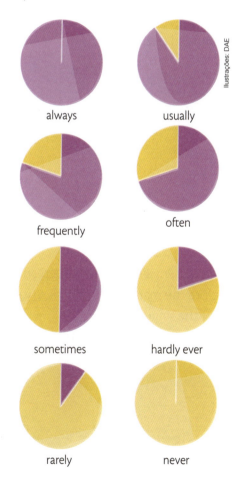

- The adverbs of frequency are usually used <u>before</u> the **main verb**:
  I *always* **study** after lunch.
  He *frequently* **eats** fruits.

- The adverbs of frequency are also used <u>between</u> the **auxiliary verb** and the **main verb**:
  He **doesn't** *frequently* **eat** fruits.
  Do they *usually* **go** to the movies?

- However, these adverbs always come <u>after</u> the **verb to be**:
  It **is** *often* cloudy in England.
  We **are** *rarely* late for school.

Pages 43 and 44

The **present simple** tense is used to talk about:
- things that are true in the present;
  I am a student.
  He live s with his parents.

- actions that happen repeatedly in the present;
  Marcus plays soccer every Thursday.
  We have math classes on Friday.

- things that are universal truths.
  The moon orbits around Earth.
  The human body has about 206 bones.

The affirmative form of present tense is formed by the **base form** of the verbs:
I **go** to school in the morning.
They **have** piano lessons every Saturday.

However, with the third person of the singular, it is added (**-s**) to the **base form** of the verb:
Lilian **travels** to the beach once a year.
His dog always **barks** at me.

It is important to pay attention how the verb ends to form the simple present of the third person singular:
- Verbs ending in (**-ch**), (**-o**), (**-sh**), (**-ss**), (**-x**), or (**-z**) it is added (**-es**).

  wat**ch** – wat**ches**
  d**o** – d**oes**
  fini**sh** – fini**shes**
  pa**ss** – pa**sses**
  fi**x** – fi**xes**
  bu**zz** – bu**zzes**

- Verbs ending in (**consonant + -y**), the (**-y**) is eliminated and it is added (**-ies**).

  stu**dy** – stu**dies**
  d**ry** – d**ries**

To form the negative or the interrogative forms of the present simple it is needed an **auxiliary verb**. In this verb tense, the auxiliary is **do**, and it comes before the main verb in the base form. It is the auxiliary verb that receives the (**-es**) with the third person of the singular (**does**).

To make negative sentences it is added a negative (**no**) to the **auxiliary verb**.
Mark **does not** play the piano.
Mark **doesn't** play the piano.
We **do not** like going ice skating.
We **don't** like going ice skating.

To make interrogative sentences the **auxiliary verb** comes at the beginning of the sentence, before the subject pronoun.

Do you like ice cream?
Does Joe play soccer?

Page 46

Prepositions of time are prepositions that indicate a specific time such as a date in the calendar or the actual time something takes place.

- **At** is used to discuss clock times, holidays, festivals, and other very specific time frames.
  At 8 o'clock.
  At midnight.
  At 5:30 a.m.

- **In** is used to discuss months, seasons, years, centuries, general times of day, and longer periods.
  In January.
  In winter.
  In the 1980s.

- **On** is used to discuss days of the week or portions of days of the week, specific dates, and special days.
  On Fridays.
  On Easter.
  On November 15th.

||| Unit 4 |||

Pages 55 to 58

Question words, or **wh-words**, are words used to ask both direct and indirect questions. They are used at the beginning of the interrogative sentences, before the auxiliary verbs or the verb to be. Some of the most common of them are.

- **What**, it is used to ask or to refer to specific information.
  What is your name?
  What time is it?

- **Where**, it is used to ask or to refer to a place or location.
  Where do you go after school?
  Where does he live?

- **Which**, it is used when a choice needs to be made.
  Which do you prefer: banana or apple?
  Which is your favorite: history or math?

Pages 57 and 58

Each country has its nationality and main spoken language. Take a look at some of them.

Country	Nationality	Language
Argentina	Argentine	Spanish
Australia	Australian	English
Brazil	Brazilian	Portuguese
Canada	Canadian	English / French
China	Chinese	Chinese / Mandarin
Egypt	Egyptian	Arabic
England	English	English
France	French	French
Germany	German	German
Greece	Greek	Greek
Ireland	Irish	English / Gaelic
italy	Italian	Italian
Japan	Japanese	Japanese
Mexico	Mexican	Spanish
Portugal	Portuguese	Portuguese
Russia	Russian	Russian
South Africa	African	Afrikaans / English
Spain	Spanish	Spanish
United Kingdom	British	English
United States of America	American	English

Page 59

The **genitive case**, or **possessive case** or **possessive apostrophe**, is used to show possession, that something belongs to another or a type of relationship between things.

- With singular nouns, even if they end with (-**s**), like names, it is added an apostrophe and an (-**s**), like this: (-**'s**).

The cat**'s** tail is fluffy.

This is Charles**'s** mother.

- With plural nouns ending with (**-s**), it is added only an apostrophe (**-'**).
  The brothers**'** feet are muddy.
  The friends' house needs a gardener.
- Whith singular words that represent plural nouns, like collectives, it is added an aphostrophe and (**-s**), like this: (**-'s**).
  This is the most famous children**'s** hospital.
  To study is people**'s** basic right.

Page 60

A **cardinal number** is a number such as *one* (1), *three* (3), or *ten* (10) that expresses how many things there are in a group (**quantity**), but not what order they are in. It is used in counting:
There are **twenty** students in class.
My family has **five** members.
I have **three** brothers.
Joan has **twelve** pairs of socks.

An **ordinal number** is a word such as *first* (1st), *third* (3rd), or *tenth* (10th) that expresses the order in which a particular thing appears in a sequence. It is used to indicate **order**:
Mary is the **first** to finish the test.
They like to sit in the **fourth** row.
I'm the **second** at my class.
Helen wants a **third** apple.

Look at the cardinal numbers and their correspondent ordinal number.

1	one	1st	first	11	eleven	11th	eleventh
2	two	2nd	second	12	twelve	12th	twelfth
3	three	3rd	third	13	thirteen	13th	thirteenth
4	four	4th	fourth	14	fourteen	14th	fourteenth
5	five	5th	fifth	15	fifteen	15th	fifteenth
6	six	6th	sixth	16	sixteen	16th	sixteenth
7	seven	7th	seventh	17	seventeen	17th	seventeenth
8	eight	8th	eighth	18	eighteen	18th	eighteenth
9	nine	9th	ninth	19	nineteen	19th	nineteenth
10	ten	10th	tenth	20	twenty	20th	twentieth

||| Unit 5 |||

Page 74

When talking about sports is common to have questions about which verb (**play**, **go**, or **do**) is the correct one to use with it.

- **Play** is used to talk about ball sports or competitive games which we play against other person, such as: basketball, volleyball, baseball, tennis, golf, rugby, chess, cards, board games etc.
- **Do** is used to talk about recreational activities or a non-team activity, such as: karate, judo, taekwondo, yoga, gymnastics, ballet classes, archery, aerobics etc.
- **Go** is used to talk about activities that implies movement and end with (**-ing**), such as: running, walking, skating, surfing, bowling, bicycling, climbing, fishing, dancing etc.

Pages 75 to 77

The **present continuous tense**, or **present progressive**, is used to describe a continued or on-going action or events that are happening or developing now. The actions are occurring at the time of the speaking.

Structure

Main verb: present participle, it means, the base form of the verb + (**-ing**).
Auxiliary verb: verb **to be**: **am**, **is** or **are**.

- **Affirmative sentences**

Subject pronoun + auxiliary verb + present participle + complement.

Full form	**Short form**
I **am** read**ing**.	I**'m** read**ing**.
He / she / it **is** read**ing**.	He / she / it**'s** read**ing**.
We / you / they **are** read**ing**.	We / you / they**'re** read**ing**.

- **Negative sentences**

Subject pronoun + **auxiliary verb** + **negative** + **present participle** + complement.

Full form	**Short form**
I **am not** read**ing**.	I**'m not** read**ing**.
He / she / it **is not** read**ing**.	He / she / it**'s not** read**ing**.
We / you / they **are not** read**ing**.	We / you / they**'re not** read**ing**.

- **Interrogative sentences**

Auxiliary verb + subject pronoun + **present participle** + complement?
Am I read**ing**?
Is he / she / it read**ing**?
Are we / you / they read**ing**?

The **present participle** is formed by adding the suffix (**-ing**) to the base form of the verbs. Pay attention to the rules.

verb ending		rule	
consonant + (-e)	ta**ke**	exchange (-e) by (-ing)	ta**king**
(-ie)	l**ie**	exchange (-ie) by (-y) plus(-ing)	l**ying**
vowel + consonant	p**ut**	double the last consonant plus (-ing)	put**ting**

||| Unit 6 |||

Page 90

There is and **There are** are expressions that express existence of things. To mention singular or uncountable items, it is used **there is**. To mention plural and countable items, it is used **there are**. Look at the examples:

There is a sandwich on the table.
There is a book on the sofa.
There is some water in the glass.

There are two books on the bookshelf.
There are ten chairs in the room.
There are some bicycles in the garage.

Page 91

Prepositions of place are prepositions that refer to a place where something or someone is located.

- **At** is used to refer to a certain point.
    At the mall.
    At the bank.
    At school.
    At my house.

- **In** is used to refer to enclosed spaces.
    In the backpack.
    In the living room.
    In the box.
    In my room.

- **On** is used to refer to a surface.
    On the bed.
    On the chair.
    On the sofa.
    On the table.

||| Unit 7 |||

Page 107

Adjectives are words that express a quality, good or not. **Opposite adjectives** are words that express opposite meanings. Take a look:

The cheetah is **fast**.

The turtle is **slow**.

Look at some pairs of opposite adjectives:

The elephant is **big**.

The hamster is **small**.

tall	short
big	small
fast	slow
fat	thin

strong	weak
fierce	nice
new	old
beautiful	ugly

168

Page 110

Demonstratives like **this**, **these**, **that** and **those**, are used to point to people and things. They are organized into two categories: proximity and quantity:

Near	**singular**
	this
	plural
	these
Far	**pingular**
	that
	plural
	those

Page 113

The conjunctions **so**, **and**, **but** are used to join two sentences by adding more information, by giving alternatives, or by giving unexpected results. Each of them has a different function:
- **So:** expresses the consequence of something.
  She is studying **so** she is not watching TV.
- **But:** expresses contrast between two things.
  She lives in São Paulo **but** she doesn't know Ibirapuera Park.
- **And:** expresses the idea of addition of similar / equal things.
  I am Brazilian **and** I live in São Paulo.

||| Unit 8 |||

Page 122

Usually the 24 hours of the day are divided into two periods of 12 hours each. The first period is called **a.m.** and the second period is called **p.m.**
- **a.m.** – *ante meridian*. It means before noon, the hours between the period after midnight and before midday.
- **p.m.** – *post meridian*. It means after noon, the hours after midday and before midnight.

There are two common ways of telling the time. It is possible to say the hour first then the minutes, like "It is ten thirty", or "It is six twenty-four". The other way to tell the time is to say the minutes first then the hour, using the prepositions **to** and **past**, like "It is twenty-five to three", or "It is ten past one".

Look at other expressions to tell the time.
- **O'clock** – entire hours.
- **A quarter past** – fifteen minutes past an entire hour.
- **Half past** – thirty minutes past an entire hour.
- **A quarter to** – fifteen minutes to reach a new entire hour.

GLOSSARY

a

a little bit: um pouco
about: sobre
a/c: ar-condicionado
accountable: responsável
act: representar (um papel); atuar
action: ação
actively: ativamente
address: endereço
adept: conhecedor
advice: conselho; recomendação
affect: ter influência sobre
afternoon: tarde
age: idade
aim: ter a intenção de; intentar; ter o objetivo de
allow: permitir
always: sempre
although: embora
amazing species: incríveis espécies
American: Americano
ancient: antigas
and the like: e similares
announce: anunciar
April: abril
arabic: árabe
archery: prática do arco e flecha
Argentine: argentino
argue: discutir
armchair: poltrona
assignments' due dates: datas de entrega de trabalhos
attic: sótão
audience: audiência; público
August: agosto
aunt: tia
Australian: australiano
autumn/fall: outono
available: disponível

b

backpack: mochila
backward planning: planejamento inverso
backyard: quintal
basement: porão
basin: bacia
bathroom: banheiro
bathtub: banheira
be gone: ir embora; desaparecer
because: porque; pela razão de
become: tornar
bed: cama
bedroom: quarto
beer: cerveja
behavior: comportamento
behind: atrás
be late: atrasar
below: abaixo
better: melhor
between: entre
biggest: o maior
bigfoot: pé grande
birth: nascimento
blanket: cobertor
blend: misturar
board games: jogos de tabuleiro
boat: barco
book: livro
bookshelf: prateleira; estante
bone: osso
bonfire: fogueira
be born: nascer; data de nascimento
both: ambos
bow: curvar-se respeitosamente em direção a uma pessoa; cumprimentá-la
bowling: boliche
brand new: novo; sem uso anterior

Brazil: Brasil
Brazilian: brasileiro
breakfast: café da manhã
breath: hálito
brick: tijolo
bright: brilhante
brink of: à beira de
brother: irmão
buds: gomos; botões
build: construir
building: prédio; construção

c

called: chamado
camp: acampamento
cap: boné; gorro
cards (playing cards): baralho
cast: elenco
catch on: tornar-se popular
cave: caverna
caveman: homem das cavernas
chair: cadeira
challenges: desafios
change: mudança
character: personagem
characteristics: características
check: marcar
chess: xadrez
Chinese: chinês; chinesa
chore: pequena tarefa; trabalho doméstico
citizens: cidadãos
city: cidade
classmate: colega de classe
clean up: limpar
clock: relógio não portátil
cloth: pano; tecido
coding system: sistema de código
c'mon: vamos lá
companionship: companhia
compassionate: compassivo

come in handy: ser útil
come out: aparecer
contribute: contribuir
cook: cozinhar; cozinheiro
cool: fresco
corner: ângulo; ponta; canto
cost: preço
couch: sofá
country: país
courteous: cortês
cousin: primo
covered: coberto
crafts: atividades manuais; artesanato
crazy: louco
crews: tripulações
culinary classes: aulas de culinária
currency: moeda corrente
curtain: cortina
cycling: ciclismo

d

dad/father: pai
daily routine: rotina diária
dance: dançar
dangerous: perigosos
daughter: filha
day trips: excursões de um dia
deaths: mortes
December: dezembro
deed: ato; feito
description: descrição
descriptive: descritivo
desk: escrivaninha
develop: desenvolver
die out: extinguir-se
dinner: jantar
dining room: sala de jantar
dirt: terra
dirty: sujo
discharge: jogar fora

distinct: distinto(a)
do: fazer
dog: cachorro
draft: rascunho
draw: desenhar
dreams: sonhos
dress: vestir-se; vestido
drink: beber
drive: dirigir
duty: dever

e

early: cedo
Earth: Terra
Eastern: oriental; nativo do oriente
eat: comer
Egypt: Egito
Egyptian: egípcio
empower: capacitar
enclosed: cercado
endangered: ameaçado
energetic: vigoroso
energy-efficient: energeticamente eficiente
engagement: compromisso
England: Inglaterra
English: inglês; inglesa
enjoy: gostar; desfrutar
environment: ambiente; meio ambiente
equestrian: equino
established: estabelecido
evening: noite
everyday: diariamente; todo dia
everything: tudo
everywhere: em todo lugar
exchange: trocar
excursion: excursão
expensive: caro
expiration date: validade
explanatory: explicativo

f

farmhouse: casa (sede) da fazenda
fast: rápido
fat: gordo
farewell: despedida
farm: fazenda
fashion: moda
February: fevereiro
fewest: menos; o menor em quantidade
fierce: feroz
find: encontrar
first name: nome
fish: pescar
flag: bandeira
floor: piso; chão
follow: seguir
following: seguinte
food: comida
foreign: estrangeiro
forest: floresta
forever: para sempre
forget: esquecer
forward: adiantado
France: França
freedom: liberdade
freeze-proof: à prova de congelamento
French: francês; francesa
Friday: sexta-feira
friends: amigos
fuel: combustível
fun: divertido
furnished: mobiliado
furry: peludo

g

garage: garagem
garden: jardim
gather: juntar; reunir
gender: gênero

Germany: Alemanha
German: alemão
get up: levantar
glass: vidro
growth: crescimento
great: grande
greet: cumprimentar; saudar
grow: crescer
go round: dar voltas; girar
good: bom; boa
goodbye: adeus
grandmother: avó
grandfather: avô
greetings: saudações
guess: adivinhar; supor
guide: guia
gymnastics: ginástica

h

habits: hábitos
halt: parar
hand: mão
handicraft: artesanato
handshake: aperto de mão
happen: ocorrer; acontecer
hat: chapéu; boné
heal: curar
health: saúde
hello: olá
help: ajudar
helpful: útil
heroine: heroína
hi: oi
highest: mais alto
High School: Ensino Médio
hole: buraco
homework: lição de casa
honour: honra
horse riding: passeios a cavalo
house: casa
houseboat: casa flutuante

household chores: tarefas domésticas
hug: abraçar
hungry: com fome
hunting: caça

i

Identity Card (ID): Carteira de Identidade
igloo: iglu
increase: aumentar
informative: informativo
instruction: instrução
instructive: educativo
instead: em vez de
interview: entrevistar
invite: convidar
Italy: Itália
Italian: italiano

j

January: janeiro
Japan: Japão
Japanese: japonês; japonesa
join: ligar
July: julho
June: junho
jungle: selva

k

keen: entusiasmado
keep: manter
kind (noun): espécie (substantivo)
kind (adjective): bondoso (adjetivo)
kiss: beijo
knowledge: conhecimento
kitchen: cozinha

l

label: classificar; marcar
labour: trabalho
last name/surname: sobrenome
landmark: marco
landscape: paisagem
largely: amplamente
largest: o maior
late: tarde
law: lei
lbs: libras (unidade de medida equivalente a 453,59 gramas)
learn: aprender
leaves: folhas
leisure: lazer
lessen: diminuir
lie: repousar
lift down: descer
lift up: levantar
light: luz
listen: ouvir
literal: literal; ao pé da letra
live: viver
location: local
logging: exploração madeireira
long run: longo prazo
longest: o mais longo
look like: parecer
lowland: planície
loyal: fiel
lunch: almoço

m

maintenance: manutenção
major: principal
make: fazer
March: março
match: combinar; igualar
May: maio
meal: refeição
mean: meio

meaning: significado
meet: encontrar
member: membro
mess: bagunça
method: método
Mexico: México
Mexican: mexicano
microwave oven: forno de micro-ondas
mild: moderado
mimic: imitar
missing: que falta
mobile home: casa móvel (trailer)
mom/mother: mãe
momentum: impulso; ânimo; ritmo
Monday: segunda-feira
monument: monumento
morning: manhã
mountain: montanha
movie: filme
mud: lama

n

namaste: saudação respeitosa da Índia; significa "eu me curvo a você"
narrative: narrativo
nationality: nacionalidade
need: necessidade
neighbor: vizinho
never: nunca
New Zealand: Nova Zelândia
nice: legal; bacana
nickname: apelido
night: noite
nightmare: pesadelo
notebook: caderno
North: Norte
Northern: nativo do Norte
November: novembro
nowadays: atualmente

o

obey: obedecer
occupation: ocupação; trabalho
October: outubro
offer: oferecer
often: frequentemente
old: velho; antigo
on the way: a caminho
onto: em cima
organizer: organizador
other: outro
ourselves: nós mesmos
outside: do lado de fora
overprotective: superprotetor
own: próprio
owner: dono

p

pair: dupla; par
paint: pintar
pamphlet: panfleto
pan: panela
parents: pais
parking: estacionamento
per week: por semana
perform: fazer; realizar
permanent workers: trabalhadores permanentes
persuasive: persuasivo
Peruvian: peruano
planner: cronograma; lista de afazeres
plate: prato
play: brincar; jogar; tocar
plus: mais; em adição
pole: estaca
Portuguese: português
price: preço
principle: princípio
previous: anterior
problem: problema
professional: profissional

provide: fornecer
push up: impulsionar
pyramids: pirâmides

q

quiet: calmo; silencioso

r

rake leaves: limpar as folhas que caem das árvores
rarely: raramente
read: ler
reclaimed wood: madeira reciclada
recreational games: esportes recreativos
refrigerator: geladeira
relationship: relacionamento
relative: parente
relax: relaxar
report: relatório; notícia
report card: boletim
research: pesquisar
respectful: respeitoso
responsible: responsável
review: resenha
riddle: charada; adivinha
ride: andar por; viajar por meio de transporte; montar a cavalo
right: certo
river: rio
rhyme: rima; verso
roam: vaguear; ocupar
rock: pedra
roller skating: patinação
rope: corda
routine: rotina
rug: tapete
rule: regra
rule: governar
running: corrida

s

sand: areia
sandcastle: castelo de areia
Saturday: sábado
say: dizer; falar
scar: cicatriz
school: escola
scout: escoteiro
seasons: estações do ano
second/middle name: nome do meio
sections: seções
security deposit: depósito de segurança
sell: vender
sentence: frase
September: setembro
share: dividir
shelf: estante; prateleira
shelter: abrigo
ship: navio
short: curto; pequeno
show: demonstrar
shower: chuveiro
shutters: persianas
sick and tired (expression): cansada; farta; sem disposição
sink: pia
sister: irmã
sit: sentar
sleep: dormir
slip out: sumir; desaparecer
slow: devagar
small: pequeno
smel: sentir o cheiro; cheirar
snack: lanche; petisco
soccer: futebol
soil: solo
sometimes: algumas vezes
son: filho
South: Sul
Southern: nativo do Sul
Spain: Espanha

Spanish: espanhol
speak: falar
spherical: esférico
spiritual: espiritual
spring: primavera
stand: levantar; ficar em pé
start: começar; iniciar
statement: afirmação; declaração
steel: aço
sticky-note flags: notas adesivas de papel
stilt: estaca
stone: pedra
stop: parar
story: história
stove: fogão
straw bale: fardo de palha
strengthening: fortalecimento
strong: forte
summer: verão
summer camp: colônia de férias de verão
Sunday: domingo
support: apoio; sustento
surface: superfície
surroundings: arredores
swarm: fervilhar
swim: nadar

t

table: mesa; tabela
take: pegar
take place: acontecer
talk back: responder; falar de volta
tall: alto
tallest: mais alto
teeth: dentes
teenage: adolescente
tell: contar; falar
tent: barraca
thank you/thanks: obrigada
thin: magro

thought: pensamento
threats: ameaças
thrifty: econômico
through: através
Thursday: quinta-feira
time zones: fusos horários
title: título
to be trusted: ser confiável
together: junto
toilet seat: tampa do vaso sanitário
toy: brinquedo
tree: árvore
trustworthy: confiável
truth: verdade
Tuesday: terça-feira
turn: vez
tyres: pneus

u

uncle: tio
under: sob
unfurnished: não mobiliado
useful: útil
uninhabited: desabitado
United States of America: Estados Unidos da América
unscramble: pôr em ordem
utilities: serviços

v

vacation: férias
value: valor
vegetable: legumes; hortaliças
vehicle: veículo

w

wake up: acordar
wall: muro; parede
want: querer
wardrobe: guarda-roupa

warm: morno
wash: lavar
watch: assistir
water activities: atividades aquáticas
waterfront: beira-mar
weak: fraco
wear: vestir
weather: clima; tempo
way too: muito
weekend: final de semana
Wednesday: quarta-feira
welcome: dar boas vindas
western: ocidental; nativo do ocidente

whisper: cochicho; murmúrio
whistles: assobios
whom: quem; que
wicker ball: bola de vime
wild: selvagem
wind: vento
winter: inverno
within: dentro dos limites; ao alcance
without: sem
word: palavra
work: trabalho
worried: preocupado
written: escrito
wrong: errado

x

y

younger: mais novo
yourself: si mesmo(s)
youth: juventude
yurt: tipo de cabana tradicional; com estrutura de madeira coberta por feltro, lã ou couro; usada por povos da ásia central

z

zoo: zoológico